Terra Nullius: The Rebirth of a Land Without Peace

Terra Nullius: The Rebirth of a Land Without Peace

Noor Dahri

Vij Books India Pvt Ltd
New Delhi (India)

Published by

Vij Books India Pvt Ltd
(Publishers, Distributors & Importers)
2/19, Ansari Road
Delhi – 110 002
Phones: 91-11-43596460, 91-11-47340674
Fax: 91-11-47340674
e-mail: vijbooks@rediffmail.com
web : www.vijbooks.com

Copyright © 2019, *Author*

ISBN: 978-93-88161-74-9 (Paperback)

ISBN: 978-93-88161-75-6 (ebook)

CONTENTS

ACKNOWLEDGEMENT

I would like to acknowledge my great debt of gratitude to everyone who has made this volume possible. First, of course, I must thank to Luke Akehurst, director of 'We Believe in Israel', who granted a permission to add its booklet written by Professor Alan Johnson as a last chapter in my book.

I am also grateful to Chief Superintendent (Rt) Asher Ben Artzi, who served more than 30 years in the Israeli police and the Shin Bet, the Israeli security agency, for his review and also to Dr Nancy Kobrin, who is specialised in Early Childhood Development – Jihadi, for her review of the book. I do not consider them as reviews but trust and enforcement on my research work.

I am also indebted, as always, to my best friend Paul Charney, Chairmain, Zionist Federation UK, who by his organisation arranged my official trip to Israel, along with my family that helped me in understanding the Israeli diverse society which lives side by side without any racism and prejudice. I learned so much from this trip and would never forget his favour.

Finally, I am very much thankful to my family, especially to my wife Farah Qureshi, who guided and supported me throughout my journey towards understating the facts about Israel and the Jewish nation. Without her enormous support, this book would never have been completed.

– Author

INTRODUCTION

This is not a book, but a journey to find the truth, what I learned, found and researched for more than two years. I started supporting Israel's right to defend itself and her nation since 2014 when it launched the Operation Protective Edge. In the month of July 2014, I began to find out the truth about what exactly happens in Israel and why the world media turns against Israel.

Israel is the only land in the world which is widely noticeable than any other land so far. It is widely covered by the world media as well as the media of the Islamic world. The international media portrays Israel as a country that occupied most of its land and that it is the country that spreads terror around the world.

When I found the truth, I started writing articles in Israeli newspapers to educate the rest of my Muslim nation. But, when I proclaimed my adherence to the Zionist Federation UK, the world quickly changed around me. I became unknown to those who were known to me for years and years. I kept my effort in participating in the social media discourse and writing my articles and Op-Eds in different papers such as The Jerusalem Post, The Times of Israel, The Jewish Telegraph, The Jerusalem-Online and many more print and online newspapers of Israel.

This is the first book of mine on this topic and through reading the book, people will ascertain and know how powerful the truth is. This book will prompt those people in my community who are still hiding behind the veil and are scared of telling the truth due to fear of the people around them. Through this book, I invite those people living in Pakistan or the Pakistani community living in the UK to step out, defeat your fear and raise the voice of truth, because this is what I did.

In the book, I covered mostly all questions and queries people have in their minds or face when engaged in dialogue with anti-Israel and anti-Semitic activists. I have provided a cracking opportunity for my Pakistani community to read the book and understand the situation of the Pal-Israel conflict from the eyes of a Pakistani Muslim. Peace and relations between the state of Israel and the State of Pakistan is a powerful idea, together we will work hard to normalise these relations and create a peaceful and a mutually beneficial atmosphere where both nations will feel safe and secure meet and work together.

I received numerous emails, text messages, and social media requests imploring me to circulate my view, more widely, since the perspective I presented in my articles. When I finalised to establish my previous organisation (Pakistan Israel Alliance), I decided to publish my articles written especially for this volume in a short book, in order to make them more widely available in an easily accessible format, and to respond to the often erroneous and biased.

This is a short guide aimed at helping Pakistani Muslims of the UK and around the world to understand the brief introduction of Zionism and the current burning issue of Pal-Israel. In addition, parameters for identifying genuine facts of Israel's multi-cultural and multi-religious society as well as misinformation regarding the state of Israel and Jews have been presented. This information in the way of publishing this book should enable the reader to recognise and be wary of hate propaganda spread by the international media and the Arabs hateful network against the peaceful nation of Israel.

In Chapter 1, I especially highlighted the behind the curtain relations between Israel and Pakistan that the Pakistani community is unaware of. The Pakistani establishment and politicians always covered these relations from their own public as well as from the entire world. Israel always seeks stronger relations with Pakistan but it was Pakistan that did not want to take the risk to put the country in chaos because of Mullahcracy. These relations were already developed since the creation of

Pakistan and they grew with time but remained hidden from the public eye. The Pakistani establishment, as well as political leadership, sustained their objectives, whether national or personal. The readers will read the facts behind these hidden but strong relations between both states.

In Chapter 2, I have covered the world's most sensitive topic on the world's most infamous army, the IDF (Israel Defence Force). The IDF is very infamous in the world media due to their operations, whether these operations are in Gaza, West Bank, Syria, Iran or Lebanon, they are widely covered by the international media as well as the international community. I have not mentioned the entire role of IDF operations but covered the last Israel-Hamas war in 2014 in which nearly two thousand people died and the world started blaming these deaths on the IDF. I argue that the IDF does not deliberately target civilians or the civilian infrastructure anywhere in the world. I have stated facts that the IDF's Operation Protective Edge was not against Palestinians but against Hamas, the organisation that runs the Gaza strip and that is recognised as a terrorist organisation. I have also mentioned the IDF's code of ethics which prevents them to target civilians at any cost.

In Chapter 3, I have condemned by providing facts that the Pakistani community is not only anti-Zionism but is anti-Semitic as well. There were thousands of Jewish families that were living in Pakistan for centuries left the country, their houses and businesses due to the fear of persecution. Their places of worship were changed into cinemas and restaurants and their graveyards were destroyed along with their ancient history. I have highlighted their anti-Semitic actions as well as the mentality.

In Chapter 4, I talk about the Palestinian terrorism in Israel. When pointing out Palestinian terrorism, I do not condemn the entire peaceful community of the Palestinians living in Israel or in the occupied territories, but ONLY those who use the identity of Palestinians and commit acts of terrorism by deliberately targeting the civilian infrastructure of Israel. I have also condemned those Palestinians who supported the terrorism. I have proved that

Hamas is not a resistance movement or Islamic organisation but a terrorist organisation of the Kharijites.

In Chapter 5, I did not only condemn the Palestinians' criminal actions (burning the trees and agriculture lands in Israel) but theologically rejected such acts because these acts cannot be justified in Islam whatsoever. Therefore, these acts come under terrorism and should be dealt with according to Law. Second, I have supported the ban of the call for prayers in Mosques openly by using loudspeakers. I have provided facts and examples that many Islamic countries have applied these laws to minimise the loudspeaker when using it for the call for prayers due to the disturbance of non-Muslims living around as well as concerns regarding noise pollution.

In Chapter 6, I have mentioned the historical background of how Muslims had fruitful and strong relations with the Jewish community and how they historically supported each other and lived together. And that Islam fully supports Muslim and Jewish interfaith relations which are mentioned in the holy Quran and in other Islamic texts as examples as well in a Muslim History.

In Chapter 7, readers will learn about how the international community has become biased against the state of Israel when they pass every other resolution against her. There are many Muslim countries that violated human rights as well as children's rights but the International community kept silence or do little to condemn them in comparison to Israel. Israel is the only country in the Middle East that has more human rights than any other Arab country in the region. Israel has not violated human rights and has more freedom for minorities than any Muslim country in the world. I have mentioned a few facts about the bias attitude of the international community.

In Chapter 8, I have added thorough but a short research article written by Professor Alan Johnson, who has penned the research in a way of Q & A's with facts and evidence. The areas he covered are the most famous in the media in the debate on the Israel-Palestinian conflict. People have less knowledge about the history and facts behind the conflict, especially on the topic of Gaza, Peace between both nations, and Zionism. Professor Alan answered almost all questions that arise in the mind of an ordinary person who is interested in studying the Israel-Palestinian conflict.

To further their own political and religious agendas, these networks use journalism, print and media to foster negativity and hatred against the small population of the world, innocent, ordinary and peaceful Israelis going about their daily lives who despise and hate the terrorist as much as anyone else hates and despise them, if not more so.

It is hoped that greater awareness of what I provided in this book against Anti-Semitism and Anti-Israel groups and their ideologies along with an accurate analysis of its true factors, causes and influences, will lead to credible measures being adopted to combat it effectively.

Thank you for reading the book.

Noor Dahri
Founder & Executive Director
Islamic Theology of Counter Terrorism (ITCT)
United Kingdom
May 2019

CHAPTER 1

THE RELATIONS BEHIND THE CURTAIN

Pakistan is an ideological country, as is the State of Israel. In the 20th century, only two countries emerged on the map of the earth in the name of Religion; the Islamic State of Pakistan and the Jewish State of Israel. Both countries have nuclear technology and both have not yet ratified the NPT (Nuclear Non-Proliferation Treaty). This action shows that both states do not want to restrain their nuclear capability and always want to be seen to be tough for the enemy of the states. Israel and Pakistan never ever wanted their destruction through striking each other and, on many occasions, not only cooperated but divvied up their combined intelligence issues.

According to the report conducted by Azriel Bermant: "Pakistan is the first Muslim state with a nuclear weapons program, it does not call for Israel's destruction or sponsor terror attacks against Israel". History has shown that Israel never wanted her enemies and constantly desired to hold close and solid links with those nations who still want her destruction.[1] Israel has been the first Jewish state to offer a peaceful handshake with Pakistan just after her independence. Pakistan and Israel are historical twins and there are many political and religious similarities and coexistence.

Late Pakistani General and Dictator Muhammad Zia-ul-Haq said: "Pakistan is like Israel, an ideological state, take out the Judaism from Israel and it will fall like a house of cards. Take Islam

---

1   Details of Azriel Bermant Report.

out of Pakistan and make it a secular state; it would collapse." General Zia-ul-Haq wanted bilateral relations with Israel, and in fact, he established secret intelligence cooperation with Israel over different operations. Despite the nation of Pakistan, the government of Pakistan does not hate Israel at all because Pakistan accepts the powerful growth and Israeli influence in the world. Pakistan always seeks help and Israeli cooperation whenever it is needed and, on many political matters, Israel unconditionally has helped Pakistan. Israel has always wanted good relations with Pakistan since its birth.[2]

The actual intention of writing this article is to bring to the Pakistani nation the reality that is the State of Israel. Pakistani political leaders, army generals, diplomats, journalists and the establishment have always wanted a good relationship with the State of Israel - which is a good outcome, but, regrettably, the fear of radical Mullahs or an extremist type nation did not pull in these pillars in order to step forward towards Israel. Pakistan and the Pakistani nation are branded as a land and country of terrorism by the international community, and now Pakistan has a prime opportunity to shed this label with the help of Israel and to show the world that Pakistan is ready and more capable to nurture and preserve these historical links.

Pakistan could help solve the Palestine issue with the assistance of Israel because Palestine and other Arab countries see Pakistan as a most valuable, dependable and reliable state. Palestine is a political issue instead of a religious one and it could be resolved by political efforts. Pakistan has the ability to solve this more complex matter if it maintains good and equal relations with the State of Israel.

Israel has always called for positive steps to shake hands with Pakistan and Pakistan has also joined forces with Israel in sensitive issues; it turns out that it is in Pakistan's national interest to go with Israel publicly.

The country of Israel is a reality and as eligible as Pakistan, and

---

2   Washington Post, 13 December 2014

the country of Israel is as powerful and nuclear as Pakistan. There are many similarities and common perceptions between both countries, so let's work together and get the peace regardless of religious belief, race, colour and hatred. Israel has never been Pakistan's enemy and has always offered good wishes for Pakistan because Israel knows that Pakistan is a bright reality and she has always welcomed the call from Pakistan. Moreover, good relations with Israel could help Pakistan to improve its shape in the eyes of the international political community.

The Pakistani nation is under the horrific influence of the extreme Mullah Mafia who does not want it's nation to move forward and make good ties with the International community; especially with the State of Israel although Israel never posed any political or security threat to Pakistan. Pakistan cannot achieve its political goals without the assistance of Israel and Israel is the only country to have a strong influence through her solid political connection in the US politics. Pakistan has succeeded in many political goals with the assistance of the advocated American Jews in Congress. According to Pirzada Hasaan Hashmi: "Israel has the strongest lobbying powers in the world". If Israel and Pakistan are on good terms, we can use this lobbying to foster healthy relationships with other countries, because other than Saudi Arabia [and China], no major country supports Pakistan".[3]

In the era of the ex-military chief and former president of Pakistan, Pervez Musharraf, Pakistan had maintained very powerful relations with Israel but it did not go forward due to pressure from Pakistan's extreme religious parties. Nowadays, there is one prime similarity between Pakistan and Israel; both countries are at war with Islamic terrorism and they are both fighting the disease of religious extremism which has severely impacted their respective image as well as affects their wider status on the world stage

The Pakistani nation has ascended in the 21st century through social media and there are many people in the nation who have openly demonstrated their support and solidarity with Israel.

---

3   The Independent, 13 February 2013

They are very keen to establish political relations and move beyond the hatred. This more mature population, however, is still in the minority because of religious extremists' influence in the society of Pakistan, who can tolerate relations with India at some point but who have no word in their religious dictionary to pursue and establish close relations with the Jewish State of Israel. The people of the country are a tangible power and they can alter the destiny of the country.

The people of Pakistan need to step up to the plate and send a strong message to the religious community, challenging and changing its hateful and insightful behaviour towards non-Muslim states. It needs a revolutionary change in Pakistan which can bring a real Islamic and democratic country. Political Islam has put the country into a catastrophic situation in the world. The State of Pakistan should take a bold step by not only making close relations with Israel, but also recognising the State of Israel without any religious fear - because recognition of the State of Israel would not harm any religious virtue. Turkey has not only recognised the State of Israel but also has very substantial military and intelligence cooperation with Israel, which has made Turkey a very strong country economically as well as politically in the world.

Pakistan and Israel's Secret Diplomacy

My article received worldwide noticeable appreciation, which gave me the courage to highlight the same issue with a different perspective. What I argued, was my understanding of the state of Israel and its unofficial diplomatic approach towards Pakistan, which also received thousands of appreciative comments on social media. I received numerous text messages and emails on my scientific approach. In this article, I laid out the evidence, that today or tomorrow, Israel and Pakistan will openly accept each other as friends. The fact of the matter is that how Pakistani governmental and political leaders not only tried to start an open relationship with Israel but secretly visited the country times and again.

These political relations started immediately after the creation of Israel in 1948, when the Prime Minister of Israel Ben Guerin sent a telegram to the founder of Pakistan Muhammad Ali Jinnah to establish diplomatic relations but Mr Jinnah's response was very poor. Then in 1953, US diplomats arranged a meeting between Pakistan's foreign Minister Muhammad Zafarullah Khan and Israel's ambassador to the US, Abba Eban, but Mr Khan told Eban that improved relations between the two states were not on the horizon: "... the Pakistani government does not bear any hatred toward Israel and understands that it is a factor in the Middle East that must be taken into consideration." Mr. Khan said.[4]

In 1993, during the Benazir Bhutto's state visit to the United States, Director-General of the Pakistan Army's Directorate-General for the Military Operation (DGMO), Major-General Pervez Musharraf was invited by Bhutto to join her on this state visit. As unusual and unconventional it was for the Director of the Directorate-General of Military Operations (DGMO) to join this trip, Benazir Bhutto and her DGMO had chaired a secret meeting with Israeli officials in New York in 1993, who had specially flown to Washington. Under her guidance, General Musharraf had intensified the ISI's liaison with Israel's MOSSADS. A final meeting took place in 1995, and General Musharraf had also joined this meeting with Benazir Bhutto after she ordered General Musharraf to air-dash to New York immediately.[5]

Before returning to Pakistan, Ms Benazir Bhutto sought guaranty of her safety from Israeli Intelligence Agency MOSSAD. Miss Benazir Bhutto, who was in 2008, was assassinated in December 2007. The Hebrew daily newspaper "Ma'ariv" reported Benazir Bhutto had asked Israel's secret agency, the CIA and Britain's Scotland Yard, to help protect her in the run-up to Pakistan's election on January 2008. [6] In 2007, Pakistan's People's Party's

---

4   Moshe Yegar, "Pakistan and Israel", *Jewish Political Studies Review 19:3–4 (Fall 2007).*

5   Journalist and author George Crile's book, *Charlie Wilson's War* (Grove Press, New York, 2003).

6   *Israel Today*, December 28, 2007.

(PPP) high profile leadership visited New York and Washington, DC, and then to Tel Aviv. On 07 May 2006, Benazir Bhutto had arranged a Birthday party of the high figure of Israel in a New York's expensive hotel. The hotel was fully booked that night and the bill was directly paid by the Benazir Bhutto. The top political personalities travelled from Washington DC and Tel Aviv to attend that party. Prime Minister Ehud Olmert told the Jerusalem Post. "Upon her return to Pakistan two months ago, Bhutto had stopped in London and, through a mutual acquaintance, relayed a message that she would in the future like to strengthen the ties between Israel and Pakistan".[7]

Benazir Bhutto later on met the then Israeli President Shimon Peres several times in her life and showed her interest to move forward in relations to recognise Israel. Ms Bhutto promised to Shimon that she would visit Israel upon returning to power.

Dan Gillerman, the Israeli ambassador to the United Nations, told Ynet, an online Israeli news site affiliated with Israel's daily Yediot Acharonot: "Ms Bhutto admired Israel and of her desire to see a normalization in the relations between Israel and Pakistan, including the establishment of diplomatic ties," the site reported.[8]

On 15 October 1992 Radio Pakistan reported: "In October 1995, Prime Minister Ms. Bhutto ruled out recognition because "the core issues of the Golan Heights and the status of Jerusalem are yet to be resolved." It was not only Ms Bhutto but Prime Minister Nawaz Sharif also wished to normalise its diplomatic ties with the state of Israel. He had established many secrete political based coordination with Israel. October 1988, Israeli media reported that President Ezer Weizman had met his Pakistani counterpart Mr. Rafiq Tarar in Ankara during the 75th anniversary of modern Turkey's independence. Mr. Tarar approached Weizman and shook his hand. "I have heard a great deal about you as a man of peace," he told Weizman. The two discussed the peace process and the Pakistani President expressed the hope that "one day we

---

7   Ibid.

8   Ynet, an online Israeli news site affiliated with Israel's daily Yediot Acharonot

will meet again." ...[9]

There are indications that during his first term in office (1990-93), Prime Minister Nawaz Sharif was keen to re-examine Pakistan's policy toward Israel and even contemplated recognition and normalisation. A few months after Sharif assumed office, Maulana Ajmal Qadri, chief patron of Jamiat-e-Ulema-e-Islam (a party that advocates the adoption of a constitution based on Sunni Islamic teachings), visited Israel. Upon returning home, "in the larger interest of Palestine", he called for Pakistani recognition of Israel. He also advised the Prime Minister that:

"Pakistan should not fight another's war (his indication was for Palestinians organisations)" A religious delegation with the special permission of the Prime Minster office visited Israel and spent six days in the state. According to the Israeli newspaper Ma'ariv: In August 1997, the Israeli media reported that a delegation of religious leaders from Pakistan spent a week in Israel. Besides visiting Islamic holy sites, they also met foreign ministry officials and endorsed the idea of promoting Islamic tourism from Pakistan. Notwithstanding, Prime Minister Nawaz Sharif's then senior aide Sidiq-ul-Farooq gave interview in The Muslim on 29th Sep 1997, where he declared that "there was 'no harm' in Pakistan recognizing the Jewish state".[10]

After the Oslo accords, Pakistan was ready to move forward in recognition of Israel. Pakistani diplomatic officials met Israeli delegations in various parts of the world. Such kind of visit was organised in India, according to the Israeli ambassador in New Delhi that "his country was discussing recognition with Pakistan".[11]

Israeli diplomats not only met Pakistani politicians but also visited Pakistan with their foreign passports and their entire visits were to maintain close and open political relations between both Nations. Israel has never left any prime chance to fill the gap

9   Radio Pakistan, 15 October 1992

10   *Times of Israel*, 14 February 2016

11   Daily *The Muslim*, 27th Dec 1997

with Pakistan.

Well-known Jewish organisations were also keen to establish these ties and tried very hard to stable peaceful relations of both countries. In 1993, a representative of the American Jewish Committee met with the ambassadors of Pakistan in Washington and the US, not only this BUT the Vice President of the World Jewish Organisation Mr Isi Leibler visited Islamabad, Pakistan from February 12 to 16 and foreign ministries of Israel, Australia and the US state department coordinated this visit.[12]

Mr Leibler also met a Pakistani politician, Chief Minister (Punjab) and brother of Pakistani Prime Minister, Mr Shahbaz Sharif and the meeting was arranged by Pakistani ambassador Sayyidah Abida Hussein. At the end of the meeting, the two agreed that further contacts between them would be arranged via Pakistan's ambassador (high commissioner) in London.[13]

On 16 March 1993, Israel's vice consul general, Mark Sofer Zaki, planned to arrange a meeting between Pakistani Prime Minister Nawaz Sharif and Israeli Foreign Minister Shimon Peres in Devos but at that time the plan had fallen through because there were numerous Pakistani journalists in town.[14] A Pakistani Newspaper revealed that in 1993, postal connection was established via a third country, Israeli postal stamps were replaced into Egyptian stamps and then sent all letters to Karachi and from Karachi these letters were sent to Islamabad. Letters from Pakistan to Israel and the territories were sent via London in two envelopes; the address of the postal manager in London appeared on the outer one, the address of the letter's recipient on the inner one. In an April 1995 visit to Washington, Bhutto was asked at the State Department about Pakistani-Israeli ties. She responded that she was interested in principle but would have to ensure that extremist groups would not use the issue against her.[15]

---

12 *Times of Israel*, 14 February 2016

13 Ibid

14 *Times of Israel*, 14 February 2016

15 Defense of Pakistan, *Times of Israel*

An Israeli Hebrew Newspaper Ma'ariv's reported Ben Caspit revealed in 1997 that: "On 6th Feb 1996. Eight Pakistani media journalist visited Israel; it was the first such visit there by Pakistani media. Although he further claimed that the journalists did not come as an official delegation, behind the scenes there was a Pakistani political actor who arranged this visit.[16] The Pakistani political leader was cautiously exhibiting interest in relations with Israel". A confirmed report noted that in 1997, an Israeli businessman and Intelligence officer Yaakov Nimrodi had visited Pakistan and met with Pakistan's foreign minister and PML (N) leader Gohar Ayub Khan who encouraged him to launch commercial endeavours between the two countries. He showed his interest in telecommunication, establishing a medical centre, various agricultural issues and encouraging religious-based tourism.

According to the US report: "Pakistani politicians (PPP and PML-N) transfer their million dollars, bought Israeli Bonds and invested their wealth in Israeli bonds in the US, by doing so, they strengthened Israeli economy" [17]According to the US law, only American Israeli can buy these bonds and Israeli American businessmen helped those Pakistan's politicians investing in Israeli bonds in the US". [18] There were many more hidden connections and meetings between Pakistani Army generals and Israeli generals, between ISI officials and Mossad official in various countries to work together in making good and mutual relations. Bringing these two nations, with all their differences and similarities to each other, can only result in a Win-Win outcome, not only for each of them but a benefit to all in a much wider world context. It is a right time for Pakistan to announce officially the state of Israel as a good friend and ally and deliver the most powerful and positive diplomatic message to the international community that Pakistani nation is the most tolerant nations.

---

16 Hebrew Newspaper Ma'ariv's report

17 https://web.archive.org/web/20121011235742/http://jang.com.pk/jang/dec2009-daily/25-12-2009/america.htm

18 Ibid

Pakistan's Military Cooperation with Israel

Pakistan's secret military cooperation with Israel raised serious questions about its circumventive policy towards the Arab world. During the last three decades, Israel and Pakistan had a constructive rapprochement to coordinate their stances on the Afghan issue and exchange military information. There was a turning point in the country's foreign policy, when Pakistan worked closely with Israel in Afghanistan during the Soviet intervention in 1980s. After a successful operation against the Palestinians in 1970, General Zia-ul-Haq (From Pakistan) was awarded the Jordan's highest honour for the services rendered.

Gen Zia, who led the operation as Brigadier General deployed in Jorden at that time. It was said that in this war around 5,000 to 7,000 Palestinians were killed, although Yasser Arafat claimed the death toll was more like 25,000. The Operation was in the direct order of Jordanian King Hussein. Israeli General Moshe Dayan noted to King Hussein that: "Hussein killed more Palestinians in eleven days than Israel could kill in twenty years." After the Operation Black September, Gen Zia became most favourite people in the state of Israel. At that time, Zia was the only figure in Pakistan Army whom Israel could trust and could make good political and military relations with his country. In the Afghan war, Israel was one of the most important countries that assisted Pakistan in weapons and training to the Afghan Mujahedeen. Israel's intelligence agency MOSSAD assisted Pakistan in training Afghans near the Pak-Afghan border.[19]

The Russian weapons which captured from PLO in Lebanon by Israel Defence Force (IDF) were given to Pakistan and ISI supplied all weapons to the Mujahedeen against the USSR. Israel has accomplished many missions along with Pakistan because Pakistan and Israel are both good allies of the US. General Zia likewise, surprised many observers in March 1986, when he called on the PLO to recognize the Jewish state.

Operation Cyclone was the code name for the American CIA

---

19   *Times of Israel*, 07 February 2016

to arm and finance Afghan Mujahedeen prior to and during the Afghan/Soviet war. American CIA and Pakistani ISI worked shoulder to shoulder against the Soviet Regime. The USSR was the number one financier of Palestinian terrorist organisations such as the PLO. Pakistan's ISI had established professional relations with Israel's Mossad and had secretly passed on intelligence data to Mossad. ISI had intercepted information that Israeli civilians may be targeted in a terrorist attack in India during September and November 2008. It was reported by Wiki Leaks that Pakistan's Lieutenant-General Ahmad Shuja Pasha was in direct contact with Mossad. In 2013, Britain's Department for Business, Innovation and Skills revealed that: "In 2011, Israel allegedly exported military equipment to Pakistan via Britain; this equipment apparently included electronic warfare systems and aircraft parts". However, Pakistan and Israel, both denied these claims.[20]

In 2001, Pakistani Government through the ISI, passed intelligence to Israel about the Gulf States and the nuclear ambitions of Iran and Libya, whose programs Pakistani scientists had helped to build.[21] In 2010, according to unconfirmed "leaked" (Wiki Leaks) American diplomatic cables, from October 2009, head of Pakistan's intelligence agency ISI, Lieutenant-General Ahmad Shuja Pasha provided intelligence about potential terrorist attacks in India to Israel through Washington. According to the cable: "He had been in direct touch with the Israelis on possible threats against Israeli targets in India."[22] A few weeks before the cable was written, the Israeli Counter-Terror Bureau had issued a travel advisory warning of possible attacks against Israeli sites in India.

In 2011, Israel was alleged to have exported British military technology to Pakistan. In 2015, Israeli scientist attended the scientific conference sponsored by Pakistan Academy of Sciences

---

20 Britain's Department for Business, Innovation and Skills report

21 Journalist and author George Crile's book, *Charlie Wilson's War* (Grove Press, New York, 2003)

22 Barak Ravid, 1 December 2010

held in Lahore, Pakistan. In August 1997, the Ex- Chief of Army Staff from 1988-91, General Mirza Aslam Beg said: "Pakistan has no direct differences with Israel, therefore, was a third party to the dispute... We have no conflict with Israel; therefore, we should not hesitate in recognising Israel." Whenever Pakistan recognises and establishes relations with Israel, it will not be the first Islamic country to do so. Since it has no direct disputes with Israel, Pakistan is not under any compulsion to seek a "cold peace" with Israel, and therefore has several options to choose from.[23]

These options according to a writer P. R. Kumaraswamy are the Turkish model, it means Pakistan can recognize Israel without establishing diplomatic relations immediately, like an Iranian model, it can follow the precedent set by the Shah of Iran and recognise the Jewish state, but maintain its relationship under wraps, however, in the Jordanian model, the country can imitate the Jordanians and maintain close political as well as military relations with the Jewish state without granting any official recognition, and finally, in the Chinese model, it can adopt the Chinese example and view military contacts as a means of promoting political relations."[24]

At least in the foreseeable future, the political status of the relationship is likely to be tentative. While maintaining and even intensifying political contacts in private, both Israel and Pakistan will probably be extremely reluctant to discuss the nature and intensity of their contacts and relationship in public. Israel's Relations with Pakistan would help dilute Islam-based opposition toward Israel and Pakistan should move closer to Israel because there are no bilateral disputes or conflicts between them. In search of historical contacts between both Armies and Intelligence agencies; I have absolutely no doubt that both countries still collaborate in secretive operations and work together to achieve their military benefits in the region. Pakistanis are intelligent people who keep the country safe and strong through professional governance strategies and cooperation with

23 *The Telegraph*, 13 June 2013

24 Beyond the Veil, chapter 6, page 54

other nations.

The Ex-Army Chief and Former President of Pakistan, Mr Pervez Musharraf once said in June 2003: "What is our dispute [with Israel]? I have been saying: 'Should we be more catholic than the pope or more pious than the pope or more Palestinian than the Palestinians themselves? Is this the right attitude or should there be some change in it? There should be national consensus on it."[25] Israel wanted Pervez Musharraf to stay in power; it was Israel's national interest making Musharraf strong and in power. Israel was concerned about Musharraf's wellbeing and wanted him to remain on the seat with power in 2007. According to the Wiki Leaks cables from Tel Aviv's American embassy: "The Israeli spy chief Meir Dagan met US under-secretary Burns and said that he was concerned about how long then-Pakistani President Musharraf would survive, saying: "... he is facing a serious problem with the militants. Pakistan's nuclear capability could end up in the hands of an Islamic regime."[26]

Gen Pervez Musharraf knew that Israel is a reality and it is not going away from the map of the world, he always insisted that making good relations with Israel, Pakistan will get a political soft corner in the world. Relations with Israel could help Pakistan on the world's political stage. In his first interview with Israeli Newspaper Haaretz, Pervez Musharraf stated that: "Israel is a fait accompli," he states. "A lot of the Muslim world has understood that and I know many Muslim countries have relations with Israel, whether above board or covertly. So, this is the change in reality, I am talking about. Pakistan has to keep demanding the resolution of the Palestinian dispute... [But] Pakistan also needs to keep readjusting it diplomatic stand toward Israel based on the mere fact that it exists and is not going away." [27]

To establish good relations with Jews and Israel is a tenet of Islam, Islam teaches Muslims to make good relations with other

---

25 Islamic Attitude toward Israel, Chapter 7, page 123

26 Ibid

27 ynetnews.com. September 27, 2006

religions and Islam permits its followers to engage with people of other faiths. It is in the supreme national interest of Pakistan to recognise Israel and make diplomatic ties because recognition of Israel could solve the Israel Palestine conflict which was spoiled for centuries.

CHAPTER 2

IDF AND THE OPERATION PROTECTIVE EDGE

It was the Month of Ramadan in the UK, all Muslims were engaged in their ritual prayers, and I took the month off from my work. And then the news broke worldwide about Israel's military assault on and into Gaza against Hamas. On mass, Muslims all around the world were in grief, as they watched the live footage of air strikes in Gaza unfold in the month of Ramadan. The international media threw all their attention behind this situation and broadcast live coverage from the Gaza border with Israel to appraise the world of the 'assault' and 'invasion'. I became very distressed and frustrated because I was not expecting Israel to attack Gaza and not during the Muslim's Holy Month of Ramadan. I eventually could not hold my emotions and decided to discuss it with Eli, who, by coincidence, had just returned from visiting family in Israel.

Eli Bar-On is an Anglo-Israeli Jewish woman now living in London who has become my best friend. She was my first Jewish friend and my first real life 'Israeli'. A very loving, caring and friendly woman with a knowledge Jewish history and experience of the real Israel. Eli was the only person who showed me the positive characteristics of Israel, which totally contradicted and challenged the sketch that the world media draws for its world audience about the State of Israel.

She described the situation very effectively with clear examples and evidence that Israel had not had any intention to launch military strikes against Gaza, or harm Gazan civilians, in the month of Ramadan but, it was Hamas who had left no option for Israel other than to strike back in defence. "We are defending ourselves and our country", she said. And as a way to back up her statement she requested of me to download an Apple App called **"The Red Alert: Israel"** and she insisted that I turn and keep it on all through the night to demonstrate how Hamas was, in fact, continually attacking and provoking Israel.[1]

I downloaded the App but ignored to turn it on, I was so furious at Israel who was reportedly obliterating so many lives at every air strike. International media were falling over themselves to capture the proceedings whenever Israel fired on Gaza, but there were very few reports, and those that did were further downplayed, circulating about the hail of rockets fired over by Hamas into Israel or the Israeli named, "Terror Tunnels" dug by Hamas to infiltrate and attack under the border from Gaza into Israel. A continuation of an almost daily bombardment totalling over 11,000 rockets by Hamas, affected 5 million Israeli citizens in their towns and cities in Israel since 2005 when Israel unilaterally withdrew from every square inch of the Gaza Strip.[2]

I was very keen to find out the reality about who actually started this bloody war. I remembered the mobile App Eli had introduced me to and one night I turned it on and went to bed. That night, I could not sleep because every few minutes, whenever Hamas launched a rocket into Israel, the App went off.

That night was gloomily depressing for me because it was the first night, I deeply felt the pain of the Israeli people. Imagine! I *could not sleep* the whole night because of a mobile phone App's warning alarm going off, every time a rocket was fired on Israel from Gaza, every few minutes. Yet this was not reserved for just the night-time but any time of day or night.

How could Israeli families with little children have gone about their daily lives during the day and then gone to their beds at night

---

1   *Times of Israel*, 25 February 2016

2   https://www.idfblog.com/facts-figures/rocket-attacks-toward-israel/

and manage to sleep through the night? Endless days and nights while being under the constant threat of being hit by rockets fired from Gaza by Hamas!!!! It is so horrific for me to even remember that one night, but for the Israelis, it wasn't just for that one night in 2014 but almost every day and night for the previous 9 years.[3]

I was in a very confusing situation, it was the first Holy Month of Ramadan and I could not concentrate on my prayers. It was very difficult for me to decide who to support, my own Muslims brethren, or those whom I detested most in all my life (The Zionists)! I was constantly praying to Allah to enable me with the strength to support only the truth. I knew my decision could ruin my life in one way or the other. My struggle of preaching about the true teaching of Islam and my dignity within my community. It was as if, I was not only scarifying my life but actually committing a kind of social suicide, which would kick me out of my Muslim community. I had been preaching Islam for years and years within my community in the UK, among my friends, on social media, on online forums and blogs. I had worked hard to earn respect and honour everywhere in the world through my study of Islam and my preaching.[4]

I concluded that, determined to embrace the truth which my religion taught me to do so, I knew what I had to do even though the consequences would not be favourable to me. I decided to risk my life by facing and telling the truth, which many Muslims have less courage to hear, especially about Israel and the Jews! I began to write comments and paragraphs in favour of Operation Protective Edge on social media but I also expressed my great sympathy to the innocent civilian victims of Gaza and prayed for them to keep safe and for those that killed their souls rest in Peace. I did not, however, expect the extent of reaction in reprisals against me from every niche of the cosmos: from my religious Muslim fellows; my friends; my followers; my social media friends; and, even from my own blood relations. Those same people who always valued and honoured me and called me their Muslim brother (Akhi), turned

---

3   *Times of Israel*, 25 February 2016

4   Ibid

into vessels of hate and called me, the (then) most hated of hated: A "ZIONIST".[5]

They sent me Quranic verses in proof and justification of hatred of Jews and the need to support Hamas' resistance. I rejected their so-called interpretation of the Quranic verses because I read the Quran, I know the Quran and I have experience of these people's tactics. How they manipulate these verses to achieve their objectives of hate. My entire pursuit and reputation of preaching Islam was completely damaged by supporting Operation Protective Edge. I lost my relatives, blood relations, my friends, to whom I preached Islam for years on forums and blogs. I also enraged my beloved cousin who was my benefactor in my struggle of religious learning, whom I always considered as my elder brother (**Lalabha**). They all issued a verbal fatwa (Verdict) against me. But in the dark times there has been just one individual who lit up the gloom, who stood firm beside me and with me, who vehemently supported me when I was abandoned and became alone.

The one who always encouraged me that I was right and that Allah was with me because I supported all innocent people and stood against all oppressors. That was my beloved wife **Farah Qureshi**. She understood the whole situation. I described it to her and she boosted me up to take a step forward with my Jewish brothers and sisters who have suffered for thousands of years. They really needed our support; they needed someone who would speak out about them and someone who feels their pain.

My Muslim brothers and sisters who were constantly in touch with me in regard to asking queries about Islam now call me names. "Israeli agent", an "Infidel", a "Zionist". It was not comfortable for me to absorb all this hate directed at me but I remained patient and asked Allah for help.

I continue concentrating on Israel and Palestinian's history. To learn the culture and politics of Israel and the Jewish people, how they think and feel about non-Jews generally and Muslims

---

5   Ibid

particularly. All aspects of the way of life of the Israeli people. The most basic of what I have ascertained, which has altered my life, is that they were never taught to hate non-Jews or kill those who are not of their faith. All they want is to live in peace and harmony which is their basic right granted by the Almighty. In the nearly two years since Operation Protective Edge started and my Muslim community disowned me, I have learned enough to understand about what Israelis are, what they think, how they react, what are their religious beliefs and their geographical history and, of course, their love for the land given by HaShem/Allah.

It was Hamas, who chose the Muslim's Holy Month of Ramadan to increase strikes against Israel to provoke a reaction and it was already pre-planned. It was Ismael Haniyeh and Khaled Mashal who dragged their people into the fire. They are the real agitators and implementers of apartheid. They knew Israel will retaliate with the full force of her power that would result in the damage of the whole of Gaza's economic and physical infrastructure that Hamas have neglected since taking power.

Hamas is responsible for the killing of Palestinian innocent people, not Israel. I still feel the pain of those who were killed in Gaza, who were commanded, and enforced by Hamas to be human shields during Israeli air strikes. They were the innocent who were required to sacrifice their lives for their guilty leaders so that the guilty could achieve their political goals on the world stage at their expense of the innocent. Hamas traded in the images of the dead bodies of their people to tug at the heartstrings and generate the protests from the worlds most gullible. And in doing so enabled the guilty to line their pockets and increased their own personal bank accounts with billions of dollars of relief donations.

The state of Israel has never initiated war against Gaza, the disputed territories or Arab countries, but have always acted to defend and protect the only Jewish state in the world and its multi-religious civilian population. Israel has every right to defend it to provide safety and protection to the nation of Israel. The year of 2014 was not only the year of loss and grief in my life, and a disaster that changed my Islamic social life, but was the year my eyes and heart were opened and I am very happy that at least, I have found out the reality. Had it not been for the events in 2014, I could have lived all my life in hatred towards Israel, Israelis and Zionists but I am now free of hatred. I have decided to pursue educating my Muslim Pakistani community and aim to continue working among them for the peace and coexistence between both nations which is the precise message of Islam. Insha'Allah / B'ezrat HaShem

The Ramadan Operation and Why Israel is forced to defend itself

It was the month of Ramadan when Israel launched the Operation Protective Edge in defence. Through the world, many people question as to why Israel killed thousands of civilians in Gaza in the 2014 war. They ask why Israel launched Operation Protective Edge during the Muslim's holy month of Ramadan and killed Palestinian civilians. These questions require a detailed answer, but in this limited space, I simply desire to highlight ground realities in the Ramadan War.

If we examine the history of Palestine, within the Arab-Israel wars/conflicts, we can acknowledge that Palestinians/Arabs initiated first against Israel, and Israel, then protected the country and nation. However, as a defence, Israel used precaution not to hurt civilian structure. Israel is still being blamed for war crimes, killing of innocent civilians, including women, children and elderly. These allegations need positive rebuttal and antithesis analysis. The majority of Arab analysts waste their energy in a biased analysis against Israel.

I have read so many counter terrorism pundits who analysed all terrorism related incidents around the world but when they address the Israel-Palestinian conflict, they are unbalanced in their analytic reproach and start blaming Israel for the crime that it did not commit. Every country holds a full right to secure its borders and defend its nation from any type of threat that may pose danger and risk to the country and people as Israel does. Why then, is Israel blamed always for defending the country in the same manner as the US, the UK and Pakistan do? Operation Protective Edge was launched in July 2014 against the offensive strike by Hamas into Israeli cities, in which thousands of Israelis, including women and children's lives, were psychologically damaged and functionally unstable. Israel bore no other alternative except to launch the operation against Hamas, the terrorist organisation, to deter the terrorist activities.[6]

This is why, I believe that Israel was justified – legally, morally, diplomatically and politically in responding to the dangers posed by the rocket attacks against non-combatant civilians of the state of Israel. Hamas attacks on Israel, either by rocket or through terror tunnels, forced Israel to respond as any democratic country would do, just as Pakistan launched the operation Zerb-e-Azab against the terrorist organisations. We must determine the whole scenario before rushing to the conclusion of Operation Protective Edge. The state of Israel never achieved any political or economic benefits nationally or internationally by launching a defensive operation against Hamas offensive terrorist acts. Israel merely holds right to defend her nation.

There were many reasons behind striking in Gaza against Hamas that forced Israel to launch the operation:

1. In March 2014, Israeli navy seized a ship containing rockets smuggled from Iran to the Gaza strip.

2. In April 14, Hamas and Fatah made a coalition deal against the state of Israel.

3. In July 14, Hamas openly launched rocket attacks in the cities of Israel.

4. On 7th July 2014, about 80 projectiles were fired pointing Israeli cities.

5. The following day Israel launched Operation Protective Edge to save the nation from these horrific rocket attacks.

---

6   Jerusalem Post, July 2014

6. During the entire month of July, Hamas fired more than 3000 rockets and more than 1500 mortars and the following month of August, about 950 rockets.[7]

From January 2014 to August 2014, a total of about 5000 rockets were fired at Israel. Israel did not retaliate for a few months and kept calm and drew international community's attention through political efforts. However, no positive result stopped terror attacks. Israel's retaliation was much less than other democratic countries who suffered in the same situation. The strikes destroyed the areas of conflict. Below, listed, is the monthly ratio of rocket attacks and Israel's retaliation.

1. On Jan 2014, Hamas fired 44 rockets and 4 mortars, but Israel did not retaliate

2. On Feb 2014, Hamas fired 9 rockets with zero retaliation from Israel

3. On March 2014, Hamas fired 65 rockets and 1 mortar which killed one Israeli and injured one yet Israel still did not avenge.

4. In April, May and June Hamas fired about 100 rockets which injured many Israelis, but Israel's response was simply to produce political pressure.[8]

According to a UN report: "Palestinians armed groups fired 4881 rockets and 1753 mortars towards Israel from 8th July and 20th August 2014. At least 243 of these projectiles were intercepted by Israel's Iron Dom missile defence system, while at least 34 fell short and landed within the Gaza strip." Most of the rockets and mortars hit in Israel's built-up areas and damaged civilian structure such as residential homes, infrastructure, public buildings and educational institutions. Out of thousands Hamas rocket attacks, 224 rockets directly hit civilian residential areas and these terror acts are considered war crimes against humanity. Hamas rocket attacks temporarily weakened Israel's economic hub such as Tel

---

7   BBC, 05 March 2014

8   https://www.idfblog.com/2017/06/12/why-hamas-is-a-terror-organization/

Aviv airport when the airport authorities cancelled international and national flights for 36 hours and shut the airport which cost a huge financial damage to the Israel.[9]

According to Amnesty International Report: "By the end of 26th August, the Israel's tax authority had already paid the equivalent of some US$20 million as compensation for "direct damages", including damage to buildings and vehicles." Operation Protective Edge had cost the Israeli economy almost half as much as originally thought. The most effected sector in Israel was tourism during the Israel-Hamas war, which brought down the tourists from abroad including hotel, restaurant industries and airline revenues. Many Israeli businesses in the war-torn region were forced to shut down or reduce work during the conflict.[10]

According to the Bank of Israel: "Though early estimates put the damage to Israel's economic growth at 0.5%-0.6% of GDP, the Bank's new estimate, from its forthcoming annual report, put the damage at .3% of GDP, around NIS 3.5 billion." Could any nation tolerate such type of threat to its nations? Of course not! Any democratic country would react even more aggressively than Israel had acted against the terrorist acts of Hamas. The US is now leading a coalition of nations in an endeavour to destroy ISIS, employing many of the same military tactics for which some these nations blamed Israel.

The Muslim world always blames Israel and the US for not allowing them to have their own separate state, which a widely spread propaganda war against Israel. In bias and hatred against the Jewish nation, the followers of Islam have forgotten the historical context which shows that Israel was always serious to offer them a separate state. It was Yasser Arafat and other Palestinian political leadership that not only refused the statehood proposal, but incited the violence and terrorist instead.

Below, are a few historical offers of statehood that were rejected and strongly disapproved by the Palestinian leaders?

9   Ibid

10   Amnesty International, 15 March 2015

1. The Peel commission in 1937.

2. The UN offer or partition plan in 1947.

3. The Oslo accord in 1994.

4. Camp David-Tab Peace offer in 2000-2001.

5. Completely withdraw from the Gaza strip in 2005.

6. Ehud Olmert offer in 2008.[11]

In October 2001, just three weeks after the 9/11, the President of the US George W Bush announced that: "The United States supported the creation of a Palestinian state".

Yasser Arafat refused the most generous offer of the statehood by Israel, which was considered a great crime. The offer which Arafat rejected; Saudi Prince Bander Bin Sultan called it a crime against the Palestinians.

1. The Palestinian statehood.

2. Nearly 97% of the occupied territories.

3. The old city of Jerusalem, including Masjid Al-Aqsa.

4. $30 billion in compensation for the refugees.[12]

Yasser Arafat rejected the most generous offer in the history of the Israel-Palestine conflict. Saudi Arabian prince Bander Bin Sultan called this rejection a real crime. He stated to Yasser Arafat: "Sir, what I told you. If we lose this opportunity, it is not going to be a tragedy; it is going to be a CRIME."

Now, it's not Israel who should be blamed for not offering peace and statehood of Palestine, but Yasser Arafat and Palestinian leaderships including Hamas. Israel, the US and the Kingdom of Saudi Arabia were serious for Palestinians to have their own separate state, but they were not interested in a separate state but terrorism, violence and war against the Jewish state of Israel.

---

11 The case for Israel, chapter 23, page 164

12 Ibid

The kingdom of Saudi Arabia knew that the Palestinian's political leadership was not and would never be serious for the rights and freedom of Palestinians.

At that point, when Yasser Arafat rejected the Palestinian statehood in 2000, Saudi Prince Bander Bin Sultan was so disheartened with Arafat's rejection and he asserted to him: "Either you take this deal or we go to war against Israel. If you take this deal, we will all throw our weight behind you. If you do not take this deal, do you think anybody will go to war for you?" This was a final admonition to the Palestinians leadership that in future KSA will not support them in any war against the state of Israel.

Operation Protective Edge was a need of that time when a country's security was at risk by Hamas. Israel always shows a generous humanitarian attitude towards Gaza. In 2005, after withdrawing from the Gaza strip, Israel made a deal with the PA (Palestinian Authority) to open the Rafah crossing on the Egypt-Gaza border. The deal was part of an attempt to bolster trade and economic development in Gaza for the welfare of the Palestinian people.

The Rafah crossing was open until the first half of 2006. Hamas quickly recapitulates its attacks and February 2006, Hamas fired 47 rockets into Israel and in June hundreds of local and Iranian made rockets were launched at Israel. It was a great danger and security risk for Israel to continue opening this crossing.

People around the world claim that because of Israel's blockade, Gazan people chose their survival through underground tunnels. However, people are unaware that these underground tunnels were used for many unlawful and illegal activities to harm Israeli citizens such as:

1. Hamas has no any reason to dig these tunnels from Gaza to any southern Israeli cities other than to kidnap Israeli citizens and army personnel to accomplish its political goals. For example, they were used in the kidnapping of IDF soldier Gilad Shalit and the killing of two Israelis and

injuring many in 2006.

2. Hamas digs underground tunnels from the Gaza border to the Egyptian border to smuggle arms to apply against Israel and gain illegal money for their personal benefits.

3. Each tunnel costs $3 million to Hamas and at this time the IDF had found 30 tunnels. These 30 tunnels amount to the cost of $90 million to Hamas.[13]

Hamas could have invested the $90 million dollars in the welfare of Palestinian people. If Hamas stops digging one tunnel, it can save $3 million and they could have built:

1. 86 Homes.

2. 7 Mosques.

3. 6 Schools.

4. 19 Medical clinics.

According to Israeli official reports:

"More than 2,000 rockets and mortars were launched from Gaza into Israel in the first six months of 2008."[14]

It's not only the financial damage to the people of Gaza investing millions of dollars to make a tunnel by Hamas, but it's a disservice to humans and new generations lost. Many young Palestinian kids die digging these tunnels and the loss of Palestinian's lives of children can never be replaced by money. According to an Institute for Palestinians study, which published a detailed report on Gaza tunnels in the summer of 2012: "At least 160 children have been killed in the tunnels, regarding to Hamas officials"? This is typical to what Hamas does. Hamas strategy is to use civilians, including children and women as a human shield, whether in a war against Israel or in digging the terror tunnels.

---

13 https://www.idfblog.com/2017/08/10/hamas-exploits-gazans-to-build-tunnel-network/

14 Ibid

The world must condemn these inhuman actions which come under crimes against Humanity. Hamas always achieves their political goals through sacrificing their own children, which counter terrorism pundits named it, "Hamas dead baby strategy". The author, Nicolas Pelham, explains that: "Hamas uses child labourers to build their terror tunnels because much as in Victorian coal mines, they are prized for their nimble bodies."

I follow what Professor Alan Dershowits says which is that Israelis and Palestinians have the right to live in peace. Hamas and its fellow terror organisations deny that right, and disrupt every attempt to move the peace process forward. This is why Operation Protective Edge was necessary against Hamas to weaken the terror activities and its capabilities.

IDF, Morality and the Code of Ethics

The IDF (Israel Defence Force) is the most criticised and hated army in the world. People around the cosmos, particularly from the Muslim world, abuse and make accusations towards the IDF through electronic, print and social media or in their daily conversations. They have absolutely no notion and perception of what the IDF is, what is its chronicle and the code of ethics. They defame it because it is the army of the Jewish state of Israel and because it is one of the most dynamic and energetic armies in the world. The Muslim world condemns the IDF due to a few grounds.

- It is a Jewish army.

- It is an inviolable army.

- Arabs lost the war in combating with the IDF.

- IDF involvement in operations against terrorists in Gaza.

At every level of conversation, people not only condemn the IDF, but produce false flag propaganda to demonise and single out Israel and Her army. I am not an expert on all IDF matters, but I will try my best to highlight the prospects of their ethical code in a manner that the audience realises that the IDF belongs to a democratic country of the Middle East which pursues the rules and regulations of the national and international jurisprudence. I will not discuss the IDF's history, but will focus on the latest and the current situation of the accusations and blames.

The Code of Ethic of the IDF

The IDF is based on the code of ethics which gives a rule and ordinance to every single soldier and how to exercise their rules of the duty on an everyday base. In the IDF there are many humanistic clauses which are obligatory to abide by and no one is above this code of ethics. If any individual is found breaking any clause of the code of ethics, they will be held accountable and court marshalled if found guilty. There are examples of IDF soldiers found guilty and court marshalled by the IDF internal inquiry committee or by the court of the state as evidence of enforcement.

The most humanistic codes of ethics are as below:

- **Human Dignity**: The IDF and its soldiers are obligated to protect human dignity. Every human being is of value irrespective of his or her blood, faith, nationality, gender, status or location.

- **Basic Values**: Defence of the State, its Citizens and its Residents – The IDF's goal is to defend the existence of the State of Israel, its independence and the security of the citizens and residents of the state.

- **Human Life**: The IDF servicemen and women will act in a judicious and safe manner in all they do, out of recognition of the supreme value of human life. During combat, they will endanger themselves and their comrades only to the extent required to carry out their mission.

- **Purity of Arms**: IDF soldiers will not use their weapons and force to harm human beings who are not combatants or prisoners of war, and will do all in their power to avoid causing harm to their lives, bodies, dignity and property.

- **Discipline**: IDF soldiers will be meticulous in giving only lawful *orders, and shall refrain from obeying blatantly illegal* orders.[15]

IDF Doctrine

- Defensive on the strategic level, no territorial ambitions.

- Desire to avoid war by political means and a credible deterrent posture.

- Preventing escalation.

- Very low casualty ratio.[16]

Now, let's start examining this code of ethics and find out the other community's ratio in the IDF.

If any soldier goes against the code of ethics, he would be accountable for his unlawful actions. IDF's code of ethics is formed with the respect of all religions, races, languages or nations.

This is why; Muslim, Druze and Christian communities serve in the IDF. There are around 1,700 Arab Muslims who not only serve in the IDF, but many of them devoted their lives to protect the Jewish state and the nation.

According to the Pakistani news report: To date, 363 Arabs have been killed in action while fighting for Israel. Muslims do not feel any difference while carrying on their duties to protect their nation and country. They feel secure and exercise all their personal, religious, social and national rights serving in the IDF. They align by swearing on the holy Quran that they will protect the land and the nation without being an affiliate with any anti-state organisation or individual. This is the greatest example of unity and this is Israel.

If we carefully read the code of ethics where is written: The IDF's goal is to defend the existence of the State of Israel, its

---

15 Zionism Israel Weblog, The Ethical Code of the Israel Defence Forces - Introduction

16 Ibid

independence and the security of the citizens and residents of the state. It clearly means they protect the security of all citizens, including Arab Israeli and residents, including those Palestinians who live in old Jerusalem and thousands of those Palestinians who have residency cards given by the state of Israel. Even those, who have work permits to work in Israel such as people of the Gaza strip and the Palestine Authority (PA) respectfully.

In the clause of the code, where it is mentioned about the human life and purity of arms, the IDF soldiers are bound not to apply force against unarmed civilians and still be in a defensive position when fighting against armed militias and their offshoots. The IDF and its soldiers are obligated to protect human dignity. Every human being is of value irrespective of his or her race, faith, nationality, gender, status or position. In every operation, the IDF had used a very low-level force and tried very hard to minimise the causality, but it was the other side that used their civilians as human shields. Another accusation which is always circulated around media is that the IDF torture Palestinians prisoners including women and underage children. These accusations have absolutely no credibility and cannot be judged by the accurate source of evidence. These false flag blames are hugely speared in the Islamic and international biased media, which know nothing about the strong judicial system of the state of Israel. Any type of torture against terrorists or interrogation against suspects of terrorism is prohibited by the Supreme Court of Israel.

Torture or Unlawful Killing

Every country's police and army use force in interrogation to obtain information about their terror leaders and possible future plans to harm innocent people. However, it is only Israel that is blamed or criticised for this. The people of the world, especially the Islamic world, are fully cognizant of the notorious torture stories in Guantanamo Bay and Abu Gharib prisons by the US ground forces. I cannot find any torture stories regarding the IDF against any captives. All prisoners who have either completed their prison term or released by the prisons exchange agreements are all released safe and healthy. None was disabled or injured.

This is because torture is prohibited against prisoners or terrorists in the State of Israel. I also knowledge that there is no death penalty for murders in Israeli law, even someone kills on Israeli or hundred Israelis.

Israeli Supreme Court decided that not only is torture absolutely prohibited, but even the types of physical pressure currently being used by the United States sleep deprivation, forced uncomfortable positions, loud music, shaking, hoods over the head are prohibited by Israeli law, even in cases in which the pressure is used not to elicit a confession but rather elicit information that could prevent an imminent terrorist attack. Torture against prisoners in Muslim countries, especially in Syria, Egypt, Jordan, Saudi Arabia, Pakistan and other countries far exceeds that of the state of Israel. The human rights record surpasses in Israel than in any other country in the Middle East. Yet, Israel is still accused of human rights infringement.[17]

The United States transfers their detained terrorists to other countries, such as Egypt, Jordan, Philippines, Saudi Arabia and Morocco, etc. where torture is permissible for interrogation. However, people never heard that the United States or any western country transferred any of terrorist detainees to Israel for interrogation because any type of torture or physical force is not permitted or legalized according to the Israeli law. Turning captives over to the countries for the purpose of having them tortured is an apparent violation of the 1984 International Convention against Torture.

In many operations against terrorists, IDF did not accomplish their goals by capturing or killing terrorists because Hamas terrorists used their families as human shields. The IDF is trained not to shoot down innocent and non-belligerent. On various occasions, the IDF missed opportunities to attack terrorists, because they were with their wives and kids, and the IDF refrained. According to Alan Dershowitz: Israel (IDF) was prepared to risk the lives of its own civilians in order to spare the lives of Palestinian civilians, including the wife of a major terrorist such as Salah Shehadeh.

---

17 Alan Dershowitz, 6 Sep, 1999

Even those who always criticise Israel and the actions of IDF admitted that IDF risk their own army personnel to save the lives of civilians. According to Professor Michael Walzer of Princeton University, a strong critic of the Israeli occupation: In battle, the Israeli army (IDF) regularly accepted risks to its own men in order to reduce the risks it posed on civilian populations.[18]

Many times, the Israeli Army court marshalled their own army personnel for the misconduct of the army's ethic code. There are examples of enforcement of Israeli army personnel found culpable by Israeli courts in relation of violating the army rules. There exist very strong rules and regulations in the IDF and have zero tolerance for any people who engage in any actions that violate the army's code of ethic. Recently, an IDF man was convicted in killing of terrorist by an Israeli court, even though the shooting was justifiable by many counter terrorism pundits. This is the greatest example of the rule of justice in Israel. These rules and regulations, we find hardly in any other armies of the democratic or Islamic countries.

Although Israeli soldiers make mistakes and overreact like soldiers in every army, at least there is an ethical code against which their actions can be judged, but Palestinian terrorists have no similar constraints. Alan Dershowitz said. I ask one question to the Islamic world. I ask if they can tell me any single war when civilian causalities never happened. Look at the example of Pakistan! In every operation conducted by the Pakistan Army, hundreds, if not thousands of innocent civilians died. And yet there wasn't and isn't any accountability against the Army personnel as seen in Israel. Look at the US army. Since September 11, and especially during the war against Iraq, the United States government has committed virtually all of the wrongs for which Israel has been condemned.[19]

The world media and experts need to understand and assess the situation in Israel very deeply. They should visit Israel before

---

18 Ibid

19 Ibid

making conclusions. Muslims around the world should evaluate both sides objectively and be able to decipher between fact and fiction. They should explore what terrorism is and how to counter it without creating a difference between Palestinian terrorist organisations and other Jihadi organisations. I believe, the day is near when the Islamic world will come forward to preserve relations with Israel and will eliminate all types of terrorist act, whether it is in the Islamic world, in the Western world or in the land of Israel. I am constantly working to establish a platform from where I can educate my Pakistani community's intelligent and intellectual people who can understand and assess the very complicated situation wisely. I wish, I could take them to Israel where they can see the situation with their plain eyes and feel the peace and prosperity between Israeli Arabs and the Jewish community living and celebrating together.

CHAPTER 3

ANTI -SEMITISM IN PAKISTAN

Are Pakistanis Anti-Semitic or Anti-Zionists

We are not anti-Semitic but anti-Zionists: This is a claim I have heard everywhere in Pakistan all my life. I have never experienced such lies, bigotry and bias about this issue from the Pakistani nation and particularly the Islamic world generally in my life. The modern Zionist movement started in 1897, nearly 116 years ago, but Jew hatred or "Anti-Semitism" has existed for millennia and this was the prime reason for establishing the modern Zionist movement in Europe at that time.

The Jewish people as a nation have long been the recipients of frequently repeated persecution, ill-treatment and massacre under numerous contrived pretexts. From archaic 'godlike' Pharaohs and ancient Kings to near-historic supreme Tsars and despot Chancellors, Jews have been singled out and beleaguered for the sole reason of their religious identity. Throughout Jewish history, where ever and whenever across the world minor (individual) or major (community/social/political) discontent or upheaval occurs, it reignites and releases the never fully suppressed Jews-Hatred. Jews are the easy 'go-to' culprits for all the ills of the disgruntled, be they individuals' or communities' or countries.' Jews are accused of being the cause of all their and the world's woes. Nowhere in the world was/is safe or secure against the inevitable 'Jew Scapegoating'.

At the end of the 19th C and beginning of 20thC, it was an Eastern and Central Europe's turn. Both before and during the Slavic peasant's uprising and the new socialist ideology that culminated in the Russian Revolution, Jews were persecuted throughout Europe. And while Jews served honourably alongside their German gentile compatriots in WW1, the outcome of the War helped breed more Anti-Jew hatred, as well as provide an easy target to blame for Germanic failings. All of which fanned the flames of the ever-growing wave of anti-Semitism in Mother Russia and later the Fatherland.

In the aftermath of the atrocities of the Jewish Holocaust during WWII until 1948 and the reestablishment of the State of Israel, Jews had simply no safe or secure place anywhere in the world. However, since both the Muslim Dominion of Pakistan and the Jewish State of Israel emerged on the world map in the late 1940's, the hatred of Jews by Islamists soared in Pakistan and Jews feared for their safety. Their persecution rose 100 times more in Pakistan compared to the rest of the world's persecution of Jews. Hundreds of Jewish Pakistani families left Pakistan in the '70s.[1]

They did not leave straight after the reestablishment of Israel because they identified as Pakistani citizens, but after a further 20 years of ever increasing Anti-Jewish attitudes, they were unable to stay due to this heavy persecution by Pakistani Muslims. And things have not improved in Pakistan but the rhetoric has changed the approach. The Pakistani government insisted that they leave without compensation. All money left behind had to be ploughed back into the Islamic community. Their first real exodus occurred soon after the creation of Israel, which triggered many incidents of violence against Jews and the Karachi synagogue became a site of anti-Israel demonstrations.

The majority of Jews who left Pakistan are said to have settled in Ramle, Israel and have built a synagogue called Magain Shalome.

Every day, I hear and read the lie that "We (Pakistani Muslims) are not anti-Semitic; we protect the Jews and we value their faith."

---

1   Jewish State of Israel emerged on the world map in the late 1940's, and also Office of the Historian, Bureau of Public Affairs United States Department of State, https://history.state.gov/about.

But so far, they have failed to prove these claims. I personally have heard many anti-Jew slogans such as "Cut the Jews", "Death to Israel", "Jews are Terrorists" and many more, and have witnessed various events against the Jewish community in Pakistan. The Pakistani Jewish community had no say or involvement in the politics of Israel, yet they were still persecuted and eventually left Pakistan, where their forefathers had lived, where they were born and they had made their lives.

The Jewish community has largely fled Pakistan becoming refugees in India, the West or immigrating to Israel due to the rampant local anti-Semitism and raging Islamic fundamentalism in Pakistan. There are still Jews in Pakistan and much Jewish heritage such as Jewish cemeteries and synagogues, and there are many historical and religious sites in this Muslim country. It is reported in one of the Pakistani English newspapers in 2005, "According to the Election Commission of Pakistan: there are around 800 Jewish voters registered in Pakistan out of which 427 are women and 382 men."[2]

These people hid their faith and ethnicity due to persecution in Pakistan. One of the Jewish descendants in Pakistan, Mr Fishal Benkhald openly disclosed his identity in trying to challenge the loss of a Jewish cemetery. At one point, he debated with Muslims after which he was then beaten up, punched and kicked in his face by the Muslim mob and when the police' arrived, instead of arresting the violent Muslim mob, the police arrested Fishal. He was blindfolded, handcuffed and handed over to the Rangers (Pakistan's paramilitary troop). The Rangers interrogated him and asked for his connection with Israel. They accused and charged him with being an Israeli spy (Mossad). He defended himself by trying to convince them that his father was a Pakistani Muslim, while his mother was a Pakistani Jewess, and that he is registered as a Muslim man and is a Pakistani citizen on the voting register.

Benkhald's Jewish maternal grandparents came to Pakistan from Iran and registered their daughter (Benkhald's mother) as

---

2   Election Commission of Pakistan Report.

a Muslim to protect her. After rediscovering his Jewish roots, this son of a Muslim father (Fishal Benkhald) is devoted to "claiming Jewish rights in Pakistan. The Al-Jazeera presenter and columnist Mehdi Hassan wrote the following in his column on 13th March 2013 in The New Statesman: "Anti-Semitism was commonplace among Pakistanis and British Muslims of Pakistani descent."[3] He further argued that "this is the virus of anti-Semitism that has infected members of the British Muslim community, both young and old......." I believe his hint was towards the British Pakistani community because he has interviewed and witnessed many anti-Semitic attitudes towards the local Jewish community in Britain.

The history of Jews in Pakistan dates at least as far back as 1839 when there were estimated to be about 1,000 Jews, most of whom were living in Karachi at that time. By 1947, there were around 1,500 Jews living in Pakistan. Exactly following the recreation of the State of Israel, Jew-Hatred skyrocketed across Pakistan by Islamists and Jews feared for their safety. By 1953, there were only 500 Jewish families that remained in the country. [4]

The peaceful religion of Islam suddenly became the symbol of violence and religious intolerance among Muslims towards the most peaceful and tolerant Jewish community in the country.

Pakistani Independence caused a change. When India was partitioned in 1947, Muslim refugees who migrated to the newly established dominion of Pakistan often ransacked Jewish synagogues and prayer halls on their way. Many Pakistani Jews, in turn, fled in the opposite direction, settling in India. The following year, with Israel having declared its independence, things grew even in more tense in Pakistan when rioters burnt down a Karachi synagogue to protest Harry Truman's diplomatic recognition of the Jewish state. Wasting little time, Pakistan's Jews soon began their exodus, scurrying to Israel and elsewhere.

The founding of the Islamic state of Pakistan immediately prior

---

3   Al-Jazeera Program with Mehdi Hasan, The New Statement, 13 March 2013

4   Salman, Peerzada (Nov 3, 2013). "Role of Jews in Karachi's uplift highlighted". Dawn newspaper. Retrieved 17 January 2017.

to the creation of modern Israel in her ancestral geographical location created insecurity among Jews in Pakistan. It is reported in March 2006 that Pakistan's military dropped leaflets in Waziristan (Tribal Area of Pakistan) urging the tribesmen to beware of foreigners and their local supporters who had allied themselves with the "Yahood Aur Hanood" (Jews and Hindus).

Tribesmen who read the leaflets wondered over the use of the word "Yahood Aur Hanood" to describe the enemy in the leaflets. Most thought it meant the Jews worldwide and the dominant Hindus of India. Pakistani Muslims hatred for Israel and Jews simply comes from what they have learned from their parents, elders and radical religious leaders. Most Pakistani Muslims have never met a Jew, let alone an Israeli Jew, and yet Pakistanis hate Jews for no apparent reason other than their assumed obligation to support Palestinian Muslims. And besides, they are taught it's their religious duty to hate Jews, Hindus and all other non-Muslims. A recent poll of Pakistani army soldiers showed that they would rather fight infidel Hindus on the India-Pakistan border than fight Taliban brethren in their own country, no matter what the Taliban does to their own country. Therefore, Pakistani Muslims' hate for Israel is no surprise!

There are many examples of this ongoing mind-set and subsequent impact. The prime reason for the brutal murder of the Jewish American Wall Street journalist Daniel Pearl in Pakistan was that he was a Jew. He was abducted, tortured and slaughtered by British Pakistani Jihadist Omar Saeed Shaikh. The Islamic Jihadist organisations fuelled anti-Semitic sentiments within the Pakistani community and many articles are being published in various newspapers and religious magazines against the Jewish people, as well as many books that have been written and published in Pakistan against Jews and Israel.

"Anti-Zionism" is simply another name for "anti-Jews" in Pakistan. Those Pakistanis who still claim they are not against Jews have completely neglected to prove their sincerity towards the Jewish community. I have not seen any changes in the Pakistani community towards Jews or Israel.

44

The synagogues have been converted into shopping plazas, Jewish schools have been demolished and Jewish cemeteries have been desecrated and completely destroyed. The questions remain: Why did the immense bulk of the Jewish community leave Pakistan? If Pakistani Muslims weren't anti-Semitic, the Jewish community would have no reason to leave mass and would have stayed in Pakistan.

Why did the remaining Jewish people hide their religious affiliation in Pakistan and why was Fishal Benkhald, a Jewish man (who voluntarily disclosed his Jewish connection), beaten up mercilessly by an Islamic mob, abducted by Police and tortured by Para Military Force in Pakistan?[5]

I don't see my Pakistani community on the streets raising their voice in defence or in favour of Pakistani Jews in the country. The remaining Jews of Pakistan have never called themselves Zionists. They don't even mingle with fellow Jews around the world. So, why have they been persecuted then? Their language, colour, culture and civil identity are the same as Muslims in Pakistan yet Jewish Pakistanis still feel threatened and prefer to actively conceal their true religious identity unlike the Christians and other faith communities in Pakistan.

These are the significant questions that the Pakistani Muslim community must ask themselves and answer, especially those who claim their sincerity towards the Pakistani Jewish community. And they must work hard for those Jewish people who are still living among them and obscuring their faith due to their fellow Pakistanis' religious persecution against them.

Hatred of Jews Endemic in Pakistanis

A Muslim Zionist believes anti-Semitism is endemic in Pakistani communities across the United Kingdom. Pakistan born Noor Dahri who joined the Zionist Federation in March told me: "They are against Jews and Israel".

---

5   *The Express Tribune*, Last Jew in Pakistan' beaten by mob, arrested, 6 March 2015

He felt it wasn't a surprise that Labour Bradford West MP Naz Shah had posted anti-Semitic tweets "given her background". He added "Anti-Semitism and Anti-Zionism is everywhere in the Pakistani community.

People in Pakistan will denounce terrorism but when it comes to Israel or Jews, they turn their eyes. They believe that Hamas and Hezbollah are not terrorists, however, the practicing Muslim's love for the Jews and Zionism has left him fearing for his life.

East London-based Mr Dahri has been disowned by his family, including his father in Pakistan.

He said: "I can no longer go to any mosque in my community." I published my pro-Zionist views on the internet. A religious leader posted comments against me, which went viral, saying I should be killed. People were asking where I prayed.

Mr. Dahri was raised in and anti-Semitic background, taking part in al-Quds Day and demonstrations against Israel.

"Growing up in Pakistan, I was taught only negative things about Jews and Zionists that they were devil worshipers," he recalled.

"If any bad thing happened in the world, it would be blamed on Jews and Israel." But his Damascene moment came when the independent researcher began to study modern terrorism and counter terrorism online through the International Institute for Counter-Terrorism in Herzilya.

Father of Two Mr. Dahri, who is married to Farah, explained: "I realized that the Israelis are human like us. I realized that they are victims of terrorism every day more than any other nations in the world.

His journey to Zionism began while studying and also through books, articles, videos and testimonies he researched. Invited to join the Zionist federation by its director, Arieh Miller, Mr. Dahri is now an honorary member. I think it is brilliant, he said. I really want to educate my fellow Pakistanis in Zionism.

I believe that anti-Zionism and anti-Semitism are the same things.

As anti-Semitism is illegal in the country, the Jew haters just use the platform of anti-Zionism to condemn Jews."

Mr. Dahri follows the Salafist rituals of Islam and despite it being heavily criticized by many in the West as an extreme ideology; Mr. Dahri insists Salafis can be Zionists.

"I am very religious and a Zionist- I don't believe there is anyone else like this in the world," he continued.

"Being a Salafi is to follow its prayer rituals, but not its political opinions. I pray five times a day and I read the Quran. "The Quran states that Israel belongs to the Jews- it is not against Islam."

I believe that Jews have returned to their homeland. "If we reject this idea from the Quran, it is blasphemous." Mr. Dahri pointed out that there are Pakistani pro-Zionists who are scared of raising their voices.

"I have received so many messages from people in Muslim countries who said that they have waited for someone to raise a positive voice when it comes to Zionism, he said.

I believe they are many more such as me. I have had Pakistani journalists and politicians telling me they agree with my Zionism but they cannot go public with it, as their families will be under threat.

He also believes that, as well as the many similarities between Judaism and Islam, there are also a number of likenesses when it comes to Israel and Pakistan.

Mr. Dahri explained: "Both were partitioned from the British, Pakistan in 1947 and Israel in 1948. The Zionist movement and the Pakistan independence movement shared the same goals for their people. The Pakistani people do not realize this."

Mr. Dahri, who is writing a book about his experience, added he would love to visit Israel". He said: "I hope they would welcome me."[6]

---

6   Author's interview with the Jewish Telegraph.

A Dialogue between a Zionist and an Anti-Semite

This is a dialogue between a Zionist, which is me, and an anti-Semitic person. It mimics any anti-Semitic person over the last several months in which I discussed various issues with. I have compiled all their baseless claims against the State of Israel and the Jewish nation that are made around the world. People, especially those who have less and very limited knowledge about the Israeli-Palestinian conflict, argued for no reason.

They are not ready to listen or research anything but to only victimise Israel and the Israeli people. I decided to gather their questions and to make a dialogue-based article where I answer their same repeated questions.

Here, I present a dialogue between an anti-Semite and a Zionist:

Anti-Semite: You are a Zionist, an enemy of Islam and an enemy of humanity.

Zionist: An enemy of Islam? Am I? I don't think so. I have not done anything which caused great damage to Islam or Muslims.

Anti-Semite: You have killed millions of Muslims around the world. You are behind all problems in the world so you cannot hide your crimes.

Zionist: We have been displaced from every corner of the world, yet still we are blamed for every wrongdoing!!! We have experienced genocide in Europe and in the Muslim world and still we are mischief!!! We are the smallest nation and country in the world and still we are blamed for every crime in the world!!!! You must have misunderstood. Can you provide any bit of evidence which supports your claims?

A-S: The greatest crime of yours is to occupy the land of the Palestinians. Is it not a crime against humanity?

Zion: Did we? Which land and whose land? Have you read the history which certainly was not written by Jews? The land which you call Palestine did not exist prior to the creation of Israel. If it did, can you tell me the currency, flag and the leader of the land of Palestine? Our country was lawfully created by the majority of western countries in the world, just as Jordan and Pakistan were created and accepted.

Anti-Semite: Before your occupation, there were millions of Palestinians/Arabs living in that land. You not only occupied it but you displaced the majority of them and now you claim it was your biblical land!

Zion: I think you don't know the history of it. I will tell you something very clear. In your questions, there are 3 claims:

- You occupied the land of Palestine!

- Millions of Arabs/Palestinians were living there!

- Israel displaced the majority of them!

I will now respond to each of the claims one by one.

Occupied land: In fact, there wasn't any country which was called Palestine. There was never a separate currency or a flag of your dream land of Palestine. Before the British Empire, the land which now people call Palestine was a part of the Ottoman Empire. The regions under the Ottoman Empire were called SANJAK. There was Sanjak Syria, Sanjak Baghdad, etc. The land was called Sanjak Jerusalem under the Vilayet-e-Syria until 1917. Under the control of the British Empire, it was called the British Mandate of Palestine until 1948. Then it was given to the Jewish people, which was then called it the State of Israel. It was never an independent country or state named Palestine.

According to Abdul Hati, a prominent Palestinian leader who told the Peel Commission in 1937, "There is no such country.... Palestine is a term that the Zionists invented.... Our country was for century's part of Syria."[7]

The existence of millions of Palestinian residents: According to Alan Dershowitz, it was always claimed by Arabs that Israel was allocated 54% of the land of Palestine, despite the fact that only

---

7   The case for Israel, chapter 8, page 64.

35% of the residents of that land were Jews. The Jews of the first Aliyah in 1882 did not displace local Arab residents by conquest or fear as the Americans and Australians did. They lawfully and openly bought land- much of it thought to be no arable – from absentee landlords.

Israel displaced Palestinians: The fact is, when the Israeli War of Independence began in 1948, Arab countries ordered the Palestinian residents of Israel to leave all the areas because they were going to target the civilian population (the Jews) of Israel. So, based on this request, the Arabs/Palestinians left Israel due to the plea of the Arab countries. This is a historical fact and can be found in the history books. You cannot blame Israel for the displacement of Arab Palestinians but rather the Arab countries.

Anti-Semite: I do not believe in the facts you provided because these are all Israeli myths. We are a nation and want our separate state/country.

Zionist: I knew that you would not believe any historical facts I provide. If I accept that you are a nation and a state that really deserves your own separate state, then why every time the international community and Israel offered you a separate state, your political leaders rejected it? So, please do not blame Israel for your refusals. Here, I give you some historical dates and peace proposals which your leaders threw away:

- The Peel Commission in 1937.
- The UN Partition plan in 1947.
- The Oslo Accord in 1994.
- Camp David-Taba Peace offer in 2000-2001.
- The complete Israeli withdrawal from the Gaza Strip in 2005.
- The Ehud Olmert offer in 2008.

Actually, you want your separate state to annihilate the State of Israel and the Jewish people.

Anti-Semite: We do not want to live with you or near you; we just want our land back.

Zionist: I have already mentioned before the reality of your so-called land. You can live with us or near us just as 1.8 million Arabs are living in Israel side by side with the Jewish people. So, why don't you?!

Anti-Semite: We cannot make Jews our friends because Allah forbids us to make friendships with Jews. We cannot live with you, ever.

Zionist: I believe you have no knowledge of your religion and your holy book. This is why you lie to your Lord without having proper knowledge about him. Anyway, I will provide you the explanation given in a Quranic verse in which you claimed that your Lord ordered you not to have Jewish friends.

"O' YOU who have obtained faith! Do not take the Jews and the Christians for your allies: they are but allies of one another and whoever of you allies himself with them becomes verily one of them; behold, God does not guide people who are unjust."[8]

This verse is often quoted to show that Islam is intolerant.

A complete understanding can only be achieved by understanding the whole issue as presented over all the verses and chapters and not by looking at only part of the Quran. God specifically warns us against doing just that, upholding part of the Quran while disregarding the rest.

During the time of the Prophet when the Jews and Christians were in open conflict with the Muslims, there were some Muslims who were more concerned about maintaining their alliances with the Jews and Christians at the expense of the Muslim community. The above verse is referring to such situations where Muslims with doubts in their hearts will ally themselves with the enemy.

Let us look at some other verses about this issue. The following

---

8 Holy Quran Verse, 05:51

verse regulates relations with any people, regardless of faith:

"As for such [of the unbelievers] as do not fight against you on account of [your] faith and neither drive you forth from your homelands, God does not forbid you to show them kindness and to behave towards them with full equity: for verily, God loves those who act equitably."[9]

From the above verses, we learn that we are only discouraged from befriending those who fight Muslims because of their religion. So, according to these above verses from the Quran, you can be kind to Jews, you can have Jewish friends and you can have a good relationship with Jews except those who fight with you. You are all going against your religion and your holy book.

Anti-Semite: We do not need to learn our religion from you Zionists so stop teaching us. Okay, let us say we believe in what you said about the Quranic verses. It says, "We do not make friends with those Jews who fight with us."

In this sense, all Jews are our enemies because you Israelis are in a war with us in Gaza and in the West Bank and we are permitted to fight back. It means we follow the Quranic verse. How do you see this Zionist?

Zionist: Well, I again disagree with you that we are at war with you. I can prove you wrong as I did in the above discussion.

In 1948, we got our country under the UN charter exactly like Jordan did. How come Jordan became a lawful land for you and Israel an unlawful one? I still cannot understand that. In the 1948 War of Independence, the Arab countries attacked us and in 1967, the Arab countries again attacked Israel.

In this war, we not only defended our country but conquered Arab territories as well, including Jerusalem, the Gaza Strip, the West Bank, the Sinai Peninsula and the Golan Heights. In peace treaties, we have given back most of these areas to their countries, including part of the West Bank, the Sinai Peninsula and then

9   Holy Quran Verse, 06:08

slowly, we offered different areas on the condition that we receive peace in return. In 1994, Jordan made a peace treaty with Israel and so did Egypt.

The Peace Treaty consists of a preamble, 30 articles, 5 annexes, and agreed upon the minutes. It settles issues about territory, security, water, and cooperation on a wide range of subjects.

Annex I: concerns border and sovereignty. Section *Annex I (a)* establishes an "administrative boundary" between Jordan and the West Bank occupied by Israel in 1967 without prejudice to the status of that territory. Israel recognised the Jordan's sovereignty over the Naharayim/Baqura area (including Peace Island) and the Zofar/Al-Ghamr area.

Annex II: concerns water and related matters. Pursuant to Article 6 of the Treaty, Jordan and Israel agreed to establish a *"Joint Water Committee"* (Article VII).

Annex III: concerns crime and drugs.

Annex IV: concerns the environment.

Annex V: concerns border crossings, passports and visas. Article 6 stipulates that *each Party has the right to refuse entry to a person in accordance with its regulations."*

The "**Agreed upon Minutes**" of the treaty give some details about the implementation of the peace treaty.[10]

Syria refused to make a peace treaty with Israel. In 2005, Israel gave the entire Gaza Strip back to the Palestinians. Hebron, Jericho and some other parts of Israel were also given to the Palestinians. It means that Israel is serious about making peace and not fight with you. You have now no reason to use any Quranic verses to justify fighting them or possessing enmity against Jews.

Anti-Semite: You are cheaters and Nazis. You claim you have given back all of Gaza but then blocked off Gaza in 2007. How can you justify that?

---

10 https://www.jstor.org/stable/20698413?seq=1#page_scan_tab_contents

Zionist: Yes, I agree with you that we have blocked off Gaza by sea, by air and by road and it's not our fault but the Palestinian political leaders did not leave an option except to block off their territory. Here are facts about why we blocked off the Gaza Strip:

Since Hamas controlled the Gaza Strip, they threw thousands of rockets into Israel, kidnapped Israeli soldiers and civilians through their terror tunnels and smuggled illegal arms via the sea from Iran to destabilise the State of Israel. Hamas resumed rocket attacks against Israeli civilians and increased its building of terrorist tunnels into Israel, which it used to kill and kidnap Israelis. It was only after these acts of wars by Hamas that Israel instituted its blockade in 2007, nearly two years after it ended its occupation.

Anti-Semites: No, you are criminals if Hamas attacks Israel. Why did Israel always kill innocent Palestinians, especially in the recent attack in 2014 when the IDF launched the Operation Protective Edge against the Gazan people for no reason? They mercilessly killed children, women and the elderly but only few Hamas operators. Can you justify that? Even the UN condemned your acts of war crimes.

Zionist: I was devastated that innocent Palestinian children and other unarmed civilians were being killed in a war between Hamas and Israel but Hamas is fully responsible for all these killings. It was Hamas who attacked during the Month of Ramadan in Israel. Do you have any idea how many rockets they launched during the Muslim holy month of Ramadan? These rockets were intercepted in civilian areas. Why don't you consider these Hamas brutal acts as war crimes?

You claimed: **(1)** Israel launched the operation for no reason **(2)** Israel mercilessly killed innocent women, children and the elderly **(3)** Israel killed a few Hamas operators but most of the deaths belonged to civilians.

According to a UN report: "Palestinians armed groups fired 4881 rockets and 1753 mortars towards Israel from 8th July to 20th August 2014. At least 243 of these projectiles were intercepted by Israel's Iron Dome missile defence system while at least 34 fell short and landed within the Gaza strip." Hamas used their civilians as human shields. They sacrificed their lives to give enough justification for Hamas to achieve its political - terrorist benefits. According to Fathi Hammad, a Hamas member of the PLC (Palestinian Legislative Council): "For the Palestinian people, death has become an industry.... This is why they have formed human shields of the women, the children, the elderly and the Mujahedeen in order to challenge the Zionist bombing machine."[11]

Do you really want more proof which discloses the use of Palestinians as human shields? You referred to the UN report, but you forget to mention what the UN General Secretary Ban Ki-Moon stated about Hamas war crimes: "We condemn the use of civilian sites, schools, hospitals and other civilian facilities for military purpose." And of course, when Israel hits back at those civilian sites, then definitely civilian casualties will increase and this blame goes to Hamas, not Israel. Israel killed not a few, but much of Hamas and other terrorist organisation members. You consider all of them as civilians. The facts have shown that hundreds of members of terrorist organisations had been killed while combating the IDF during the Operation Protective Edge (OPE).

In an interview with the London based paper Al-Hayat, Hamas Interior Minister Fathi Hammad said: "It has been said that the people were harmed by the war but is Hamas not part of the people? It is a fact that on the first day of the war, Israel struck police headquarters and killed 250 members of Hamas and the various factions in addition to the 200-300 operatives from Al-Qassam Brigades."[12] These are the first days of Hamas losses during Operation Protective Edge (OPE). Now consider that this operation took more than one month and Hamas members' death tolls hit more than 1,000. These are the answers to your three

---

11   The Guardian 22 August 2016

12   http://www.huffingtonpost.com/alan-dershowitz/finally-a-hamas-leader-ad_b_798429.html

accusations against Israel.

Anti-Semite: What about the people of the Gaza strip who are starving because of the Israeli blockade? Israel prevents humanitarian aid from going into Gaza, which is needed to feed the poor and to rebuild their houses which the Zionist army destroyed.

Zionist: This is the problem. You people do not study or research anything but follow blindly what the media shows you and when we show you the other side with facts and figures, you reject them all.

This I call anti-Semitism. Anyway, because I follow the truth, I will answer all of your accusations. After the Operation Protective Edge, Israel provided thousands of tons of food and construction material to Gaza on a daily basis. Here I provide you with the real figures.

On a daily basis, Israel's department for the Gaza Strip and Judea and Samaria, known as COGAT (Coordination of Government Activities in the Territories) delivered thousands of tons of food via roads from Israel into Gaza.

In a week, COGAT delivered 23,340 tons of food, material and other humanitarian products via 1,336 trucks through the Kerem Shalom Crossing including 591 trucks full of food, 32 trucks full of humanitarian products, 33 trucks full of electrical products, 162 trucks full of construction material and 548 trucks with other materials.[13]

These are totally separate from those Gazans who enter into Israel for work, who have been given work permits by the Israeli Government to earn money and change their lifestyle by working in the Israeli market. More than 5,000 people from Gaza enter into Israel daily for work and they return back home safe and sound. [14] Hamas' intent to kill Israeli civilians and Israel's intent

---

13   http://www.jewishvirtuallibrary.org/israeli-humanitarian-aid-to-the-gaza-strip

14   https://www.haaretz.co.il/news/politics/.premium-1.2121648

to help the life of the people of the Gaza strip are evident. This is the difference between those who love death and those who love life and give life.

Anti-Semite: You Zionists cannot change our minds through presenting these fake facts and figures. You cannot hide your crimes. You have displaced millions of Palestinians and how could you hide these crimes? Palestinian refugees are all around the world because of your Zionist crimes.

Zionist: I have already explained to you that those Arabs who left Israel in the Independence War did so because they were told to do so by the Arab states.

By the way, what about those Jewish refugees who were displaced from their home countries into Israel? Can't you see these crimes?! Here are the figures of Jewish displacement before answering about the so-called Palestinian refugees.

In 1948, about 850,000 Jews were displaced from the Arab countries which include 8,000 from Aden, 140,000 from Algeria, 75,000 from Egypt, 135,000 from Iraq, 5,000 from Lebanon, 38,000 from Libya, 265,000 from Morocco, 30,000 from Syria, 105,000 from Tunisia and 55,000 from Yemen. No one speaks about these Jews who left behind everything from homes to businesses. Who will compensate them, including their new generation? Yet, some people say, Jews got their country, Israel, so why do we still talk about them as refugees? Exactly, the same Palestinians got citizenships in European countries and their new generations are citizens of a western country, so why do they still call them Palestinian refugees?[15]

Those who are still living in refugee camps, why do they not go to their country Jordan which was created for Palestinians? 60% of the population of the Kingdom of Jordan is Palestinian. Jordan uses the refugee issue to increase pressure on Israel, even though

---

15 Jewish refugees expelled from Arab lands and from Iran, Israel Ministry of Foreign Affairs, 29 Nov 2016, http://mfa.gov.il/MFA/ForeignPolicy/Issues/Pages/Jewish-refugees-expelled-from-Arab-lands-and-from-Iran-29-November-2016.aspx

Jordan can accommodate the rest of them as well. There are 22 Arab countries but they don't take those Palestinian refugees back because they want this issue alive in order to pressure and single out Israel at the international level.

Anti-Semite: These people were displaced in wars with Israel; it was not their fault. So, why do they suffer only?

Zionist: During wars, people of other nations too were displaced so why don't you talk about them? Aren't they humans or aren't they Muslims? It is because there isn't a Jew behind their displacement to blame so you don't mention it. I will give you the real figures of people of other nations who were displaced because of wars.

According to the report by Global Overview 2014, the following peoples were internally displaced by conflict, war and violence: 746,700 in Pakistan, 280,000 in Bangladesh, 640,900 in Myanmar, 953,700 in Turkey, 631,000 in Afghanistan, 526,000 in India, 6,500,000 in Syria, 1,100,000 in Somalia, 2,426,700 in Sudan, 3,300,000 in Nigeria, 2,100,000 in Iraq and 146,000 in Palestine.[16]

Now, what would you say? Look at the figure and tell me which nation's refugees suffer less in the Muslim's world? Of course, PALESTINIANS and you people are still mourning for them! Can't you see other peoples? Can't you feel the pain of other Muslims suffering around you? You just see Palestinians because you can find an easy target to blame Jews for that. You people are nothing but anti-Semites.

Anti-Semite: Israel is the only country which is behind all of the killings in the Muslim world. Israel is the only country to be blamed for their displacement.

Zionist: I knew that you people never accept the truth and are always ready to blame Israel and Israelis.

So, you think that Israel is killing all Muslims in the Middle East and Israel is responsible for all problems in the Muslim countries?

---

16   Global Overview 2014

Was Saddam Husain a Jew? Is Bashar Assad a Jew? Was General Yahya Khan a Jew? Was Kamal Ataturk a Jew? Is El-Sisi a Jew? Was Colonel Gaddafi Jew? Those heads of states who were/are involved in the killings of their own Muslims are Muslims, not Jews. The jihadi/terrorist organisations belong to Muslims not Jews. The figure shows that "over 90% of the 11 million Muslims in the Middle East have been killed by Muslims and only 0.3% has been killed by Israel throughout 66 years of conflict." YET, Israel is accused of being the root of the Middle East's problems!!! This is nothing but a pure anti-Semitic and anti-Israel attitude.

Anti-Semite: I don't want to talk to you about these issues any more. I just want to tell you that Hamas is a resistance movement and is better for the future of the Palestinians. Hamas will achieve independence from Israel one day.

Zionist: HAMAS, a well-wisher of the Palestinians! This is nothing but a joke to me. Either you hide all the corruption of Hamas and PA or know nothing about these organisations. I think I can provide you the facts and figures and present to you the real face of Hamas and Fatah (PA). I know you people would not accept it but at least I can educate you and try to open your eyes.

Hamas is one of the wealthiest terrorist organisations in the world. Its members have billions of dollars of assets throughout the Middle East and in the Gaza Strip as well. Hamas leaders are millionaires and even billionaires. They have 4 and 5-star hotels, gyms, restaurants, apartments, villas and shopping centres in Gaza and in other Middle Eastern countries.

There are many Hamas leaders who were nothing and belonged to refugee camps including Ismael Haniyeh. But now they are multi-millionaires and some of them are even billionaires. The founding members of the Hamas organisation are Khaled Mashaal, Ismael Haniyeh and Dr.Musa Abu Marzook. Their wealth is worth billions of dollars. The Asharq Al-Awsat newspaper, one of the most prestigious in the Arab world, recently reported that at least 600 millionaires were living in the Gaza Strip - the same people sitting on the money pipelines there.[17] Hamas collects $250 million in taxes per year from Gazans and that money could pay for more than 339,600 Gazan civilians to have an average monthly salary in Gaza in a recent report.

The Fatah spokesman claimed that while Gaza is one of the poorest places in the world, there are 1,700 millionaires among Hamas members, hinting that the terror group imposes steep taxes on its citizens for goods entering from Egypt and Israel and that this money finds its way into Hamas officials' pockets. In 2012, a Jordanian website reported that Mashal had control of a massive $2.6 billion, with a large part deposited in Qatari and Egyptian banks.[18]

It is not only Hamas but the PA is hugely involved with corruption as well. PA President Mahmood Abbas' son has a mobile phone company which provides mobile networks throughout the Palestinian Authority. No one can open a company in a PA area without giving a commission to Abu Mazen. A year ago, Mohammad Dahlan, who used to be a senior level Fatah security officer in Gaza, filed an international lawsuit against President Abu-Mazen, claiming Abbas has stolen over $1 billion from the Palestinian budget.[19]

The world, especially the Islamic world, accused Israel of not providing enough life resources for the people of Palestine, including the Gaza Strip but they don't think that Palestinian political leaders are responsible for their people's horrible condition.

According to a World Bank report released in November of last year, the Gaza Strip ranks third in the Arab region in terms of poverty, ranking above only Sudan and Yemen. [20]The report stated that the poverty rate in Gaza stands at 38 percent. Furthermore,

17 https://www.algemeiner.com/2014/07/28/gazas-millionaires-and-billion-aires-how-hamass-leaders-got-rich-quick/

18 Jerusalem Online: 25Th July 2016

19 http://www.adespicabletruce.org.uk/page31.html

20 Middle east Monitor Report: 11th Feb 2011

of the 144 countries included in the report, Gaza was the 44th poorest, with most of the countries with a higher poverty rate being located in Africa. Global estimates say Mashaal is worth $2.6 billion, [21]but Arab commentators alongside other sources say he is worth between 2 and 5 billion as he "invested in Egyptian banks and the Gulf countries including in real estate projects."

Anti-Semite: I do not believe whatever you said and whatever you provided as evidence or facts that are generated by Zionists. We will defend Palestine and Hamas. We will support our Palestinian Muslims and will fight you until our last breath. We will get our freedom, and one day we will destroy Israel, including all you Zionists. Bye.

Zionist: Anti-Semites or Anti-Israelis will never accept whatever facts we can provide and they will hate us for political reasons but we will continue providing them with evidence and facts which are not fabricated. While the anti-Semitism continues, others continue to suffer. We will educate people and we hope if we change one mind, we will certainly change one generation. We will continue to defend our country and our nation without caring what the world considers it; we have the right to exist, the right to defend and the right to live freely without fear.

Al-Aqsa incitement propaganda and the dirty role of Palestinian politics in Pakistan

Most Arabs are nationalists, and have few, if any similarities to non-Arab Muslims, especially South Asian Muslims. I remember, once in 1990s, a bunch of Palestinians rented a house in my area in Pakistan. They had received scholarships from the local university. At that point in my life I was very pro-Hamas. When I found out Palestinians were renting a house in my area, I felt I had to meet them. The image I had in my mind was of God-fearing people, deprived, poor and religious, sporting beards and dressing like real Mujahedeen, praying five times a day in masjids (mosques). I had never seen a Palestinian Mujahedeen before, let alone met one, so I was so curious and delighted at the opportunity to do so.

---

21 Globes: 24th July 2014

I set out and hurried to their home, which were just a few minutes from my own.

I rang the bell and a tall guy, around six feet tall and clean shaven, with whitish skin like European, brown hair and a strong, muscular body, wearing a black T-shirt, black jeans with black boots and hat came to the door and said, "How can I help you"? "Asala'amAleykum," [22] I said. To which he replied in kind, before repeating the same question. "I am here to welcome you to my area and want to talk to you," I said. He thanked me for the welcome, but said, "Sorry, we cannot meet you because we are taking a rest, please come tomorrow evening." After that, I met with them regularly. I was curious to learn about them, about their struggle against the Zionists. But every time I expressed my admiration for Hamas and my desire for its victory over Israel, they started laughing at me.

Slowly I began to discover that these Palestinians were very different than I had imagined. They never prayed in a mosque except for Jummah (Friday) and Eid prayers. They thought Pakistanis were stupid, and thought of us as second-class Muslims. They rode bikes of a kind I had never seen in my city, except in Hollywood movies such as The Terminator. They dressed, walked, behaved and spoke exactly like Hollywood actors. They had not a single feature in common with the Afghan Mujahedeen who were everywhere in Pakistani cities. Every night, they drank alcohol and brought prostitutes home. Once they fought with local university students; I saw one Palestinian beat up 10 students.

After a while I realized they belonged to the PLO; they were nationalists cum Marxists. They followed the European way of life, not the Islamic one. They were fighting for their land. One time there was al-Quds rally in the city; all the business was shut and all the mosques were full of people chanting "Death to Israel, Death to Zionists and Hell to Jews," etc. As I finished my Jummah prayer, I noticed none of the Palestinians were at the

---

22 Author's personal experience published at The Jerusalem Post, 16 January 2016

62

mosque. I went straight to their home to ask them to join me at the rally, which after all was organized for their land, for the liberation of al-Aksa Mosque and the freedom of the Palestinians. I was shocked by their reply. I felt great humiliation for my people, my country and myself.

They said: "We have nothing to do with al-Aksa day, rallies or demonstrations because we do not need help or support from Pakistanis. We need Arabs support and assistance, not non-Arabs rallies or demonstrations. It is not your war; it's our [Arab] war. You are stupid people, you demonstrate for an Islamic system after the liberation of Palestine; we need only our land, not Islam. We fight against Israel for land only – if she agreed to give us our land... we have no problem with them."

Here all the Pakistani Muslims in our city were demonstrating in solidarity with our Palestinian Muslim brothers and sisters, walking miles with our families and kids on a hot, sunny day, hungry and thirsty, chanting "Death to Israel and Death to Zionists" all day, and my Palestinian friends were drinking alcohol and watching Hollywood movies in their cosy air-conditioned rooms, courtesy of the government of Pakistan. They were laughing at our stupidity and mocking at us because we were not Arabs; they felt no sympathy with us and no respect for our efforts in solidarity with their occupied people. I had seen Yemenis and Sudanese studying in my country before, but they were living with their families, studying and praying five times a day in a local mosque. They had nothing to do with local or international politics; they just studied and went back to their countries.

The Palestinians were different. What I found out was disturbing. Our mosques were getting funds from international Islamic NGOs run by Saudi Arabia and Iran to promote anti-Israel, anti-Zionist and Anti-Jewish sentiment in the country, to further their political agendas. Local mullahs were trained to recruit innocent Pakistani Muslims – many of whom would willingly give their lives based on these imams' fatwas. The government of Pakistan had continually sponsored PLO fighters by issuing thousands of university scholarships. These mullahs had never visited Israel, had never met with any Palestinian before and had never studied the history of the Palestinian-Israeli conflict. These hateful mullahs had only one concern: international Islamic funds to satisfy their greed. PLO fighters were more interested in their un-Islamic activities than in the study, they were fighting with locals and police had strict orders not to arrest them.

I was heartbroken, crushed. All my life I had been taught to hate the Jews − but my Palestinian neighbours forced me to change my thinking. In Pakistan, we are taught the lie that al-Aksa is in danger, that the Israelis are faithfully plotting to destroy our first house of Allah and that we need to stop the Zionists. What we are not told is that Jordan maintains administrative oversight of the Temple Mount/Haram al Sharif. There is effectively no Israeli control of al-Aksa whatsoever. In over 40 years, despite the constant religious incitement I have yet to see al-Aksa endangered by Israelis in any way. Palestinians, on the other hand, have disrespected the purity of the Holy Masjid several times during that period − and no Muslim ever condemned these unholy acts committed by violent Palestinians.

CHAPTER 4

PALESTINIAN TERRORISM IN ISRAEL

The Difference between Palestinian Resistance and Terrorism

I am heading to the baseless statement of every Muslim organisation and individual that advocates that the Palestinians are resisting for their rights, their freedom and their stolen land. I asked them many questions regarding the difference between terrorism and resistance, but they could not satisfy me. We cannot label any individual as a terrorist or a freedom fighter but have to examine them through a clear definition of terrorism and Guerrilla warfare. No doubt, there are 109 definitions of terrorism in the universe but the basic elucidation of terrorism is that mostly civilians have been targeted to attain a political goal. The majority of Muslim experts understand that terrorism and killing of innocent people are prohibited in Islam.

Therefore, they do not support any type of terrorism but when the matter of Israel-Palestine raises, they change their posture and support Palestinian terrorism and justify it by stating that Israel is committing atrocities against the Palestinians. Why do they have a double standard when the situation comes to the Israel? I have seen many well-educated teachers, professors, historians, counterterrorism experts and many more academic personalities supporting the terrorism against the Jewish state of Israel. This is the ideology of anti-Semitism. I call it an ideology because hatred towards Jews is their religious obligation to perform whatever the social condition of the person, s/he gives birth to hate Israel and its Jewish citizens.

From my understanding, Palestinian resistance is the root cause of terrorism against Israel, they are not any more interested in their separate state, but the devastation of Israel and Israeli citizens. Most people still do not know what terrorism or resistance is. But they defend it because it is against the Jewish nation and it is permissible for them by any means. Not only the Islamic world, but the western world is also anti-Semitic as well. The western media is more bigoted towards Israel than any other region's media. Some people do not conceive in the definition of terrorism that without a definition of terrorism, it is unacceptable to establish international tarries against terrorism. One must recognise the basic definition of terrorism, according to Dr Boaz Ganor, founder of ICT-Israel and my counter terrorism course tutor who has defined the proposed definition of terrorism:

"Terrorism is a form of violent struggle in which violence is deliberately used against civilians in order to achieve political goals (nationalistic, socioeconomic, ideological, religious, etc.)."[1] No one would believe that terrorism in which perpetrator's intention is to kill innocent civilians of the enemy is resistance or justifiable, but when Hamas or Fatah deliberately kill the innocent people of Israel, the Islamic world not just consider it resistance but emotionally support it by making it justifiable. This is a flawless hypocritical double standard of the world, especially the Islamic world.

The stimulation of freedom fighting also needs a definition to support it. Without the definition, it may not complete the aim or make it justifiable (depends on the root cause of it).

I cannot combine the definition of terrorism with resistance/ guerrilla war.

We must distinguish the resistance and terrorism; the freedom fighter must follow the pattern of resistance in order to accomplish his political end. There are many dissimilar ways

---

1   The Counter -Terrorism Puzzle by Boaz Ganor, chapter 1, page 17

to achieve the same goals. However, it must not be the same definition. Revolutionist, anarchist and freedom fighter have totally different ideological objectives and destinations. The political goal of the guerrilla and terrorist is the same but the target made them different.

1. Terrorism is a calculated attack against civilians to accomplish political ends

2. Guerrilla war is a calculated attack against military personnel to accomplish political ends

These are the main targets which made them different actors of the same field of operations. In this instance, the resistance of the guerrilla is completely different than the act of terrorism. Those who intentionally attack civilians to accomplish their political ends are called terrorists, not guerrillas. Hamas is no doubt a terrorist organisation because it attacks the civilian population of the state of Israel. Now the question arises, what is an Intifada (Uprising)? Was Intifada a resistance movement or a wave of terrorism? Hamas and PA leaders are billionaires, living in luxurious places and most expensive hotels, but the people of Palestine suffer starvation.

Again, whatever the name terrorist calls for their action, we can smell them once we match their activities with the definitions. If the Intifada is only against the military infrastructures and governmental installations, we will refer it as a movement of resistance but if their target is solely to harm and damage civilian the population in order to create fear, then it is a gross act of terrorism whatever its shape is. According to Brian Michael Jenkins, a decorated Vietnam veteran and author of "International Terrorism":

"What sets terrorism apart from other violence is this: terrorism consists of acts carried out in a dramatic way to attract publicity and create an atmosphere of alarm that goes far beyond the actual victims. Indeed, the identity of the victims is often secondary or irrelevant to the terrorists who aim their violence at the people watching. This distinction

67

between actual victims and a target audience is the hallmark of terrorism and separates it from other modes of armed conflict. Terrorism is theatre."[2]

Resistance is not theatre. It may perpetrate violence in the same way that our own military does, or by whatever irregular/asymmetric/guerrilla means are available to it. It fights for what it believes is the good of its country or cause. The Palestinian leadership chose terrorism instead of insurgence or guerrilla warfare; they know they cannot strike against the powerful IDF. So, they deliberately chose Israeli civilians, their most easy and prime target, in order to achieve their political purpose which is not statehood but a complete destruction of Israel.

The Islamic world, especially the Pakistani community, must understand the difference between the resistance and terrorism. The wave of terrorism in the Jewish state of Israel is boosting up day by day and we must not support psychologically or socially the terrorists of the state because, as we don't support the BLA (Baluch Liberation Army) because the aim of the BLA and Hamas is the same to destabilise the Islamic State of Pakistan and the Jewish State of Israel.

The sole difference between both organisations is that one hides their actions under the umbrella of religion and others under the umbrella of nationalism BUT their target is the same: to hurt the civilians of both countries.

The Pakistani community acknowledges one organisation (BLA) as a terrorist organisation and the other (HAMAS) as a resistance movement. This double standard must be stopped by any means. Terrorism is terrorism, whatever people call it. The act of terrorism not only damages the civilian infrastructure, but the country's economic and fiscal system as well. The Islamic world and particularly the Pakistani nation need to consider that the menace of terrorism is no path in favour of any country or nation, whether it is the Muslim nation or a Jewish nation. We must intend beyond the enmity, unite and fight together against

---

2   *The Times of Israel*, 28th March 2016

the peril of terrorism, which is a combined horror to destroy the pillars of the state. In summation, I must suggest that the people of Palestine must denounce the Hamas leaders in the business of killings on their soil and within Israel.

The Status Quo, Al-Aqsa Mosque and Disquieting of Israel

For decades, the people of Israel have been suffering from internal and external waves of terrorism. The state of Israel had been at war since her birth in 1948. After WW2, the Jewish People flocked to their Promised Land, which was their enduring hope for their survival and their continued fight in their hope for peace. However, the Muslims' attitude towards the State of Israel always remained harsh; they never accepted it as the birthplace of the Jewish people or as the subsequent return of the Jewish survivors from the flames of the Holocaust to their historical homeland.

In 1948, Israel and the Jewish people once again achieved independence, but her Arab neighbouring countries refused to accept Israel as a Jewish State and committed to wage war against her as a means to rid them of her. This desire to destroy Israel continues to this day, but has repeatedly failed. Over time, a couple of Israel's neighbours have accepted that they cannot defeat the most determined and powerful nation in the Middle East and have laid down their weapons to accept her olive branch of peace. However, others continue their fight, swapping conventional warfare with relentless acts of terrorism as a means to reach their desired goal of eradicating the Jewish State and the Jews themselves entirely. To do this they created a proxy nation made up of the internal, previously migrated Arab population within the Israeli borders. This proxy nation is known as the Palestinians, and their call to arms is so-called "Palestinian Resistance". However, in its proclaimed legitimism, this contrived nation chooses to bypass the constraints of legal warfare and instead to engage in pure terrorism, where most of its targets and victims are innocent civilians, including women and children.

One of the neighbouring Arab countries, who always wanted to destabilize Israel, is Jordan. Jordan was the country that sheltered the majority of the dispersed Arab population – who now identify as Palestinians – fleeing Israel in 1948 as war was waged on Israel by her Arab neighbours, and today, 50% of Jordan's population is made up of these Palestinian refugees.[3] Later, Jordan was one of the two neighbouring Arab countries that embraced Israel's olive branch. However, Jordan also plays a double, more sinister role. On the one hand, she agreed to a peace treaty with Israel, while on the other, she boosted Palestinian terrorism. Jordon's shady contribution to Palestinian terrorist activities is hidden under the umbrella of religion.

The status quo has changed over the different periods of Muslim governance of the area. The most recent status quo is under the Jordanian government, run by the *Waqf* (Islamic Trust). But what is this status quo?

Most people in the Muslim world, particularly in Pakistan, do not know the history and current situation regarding this matter. The current status quo is a type of agreement between Israel (Rabbinical Council) and the Waqf of Jerusalem (under Jordanian supervision), which restricts non-Muslims (particularly Jews) when entering the Temple Mount (besides the Al-Aqsa Mosque) and the Dome of the Rock areas. While Muslims are free to enter and pray on the Temple Mount without any restrictions whatsoever, Jewish prayer on the Temple Mount is completely forbidden. Jews and Christians may enter only to visit the area as tourists and only at limited times dictated by the Waqf, but they are forbidden from singing, praying, or making any kind of "religious displays." Al-Aksa Mosque on the Temple Mount after Arab rioting in July 2015.

So, how did the status quo come about? This is a short introduction to the Waqf of Jerusalem. During the 1948 Arab-Israeli War, West Jerusalem was among the areas captured and later annexed by Israel, while east Jerusalem, including the Old City, was invaded, captured and later annexed by Jordan. It was only in the 1967 Six-

3   http://www.israelnationalnews.com/News/News.aspx/206272

Day War that Israel recaptured east Jerusalem from Jordan and subsequently annexed it. However, the then Prime Minister of Israel, Levi Eshkol gave control of access to the Temple Mount to the Jerusalem Islamic Waqf in order to maintain a peace in the country. The site, ever since, has been a flashpoint between Israel and local Muslims.

Muslims have exclusive authority to manage the Temple Mount and the Dome of the Rock according to their laws, traditions, and practices. The Israeli police manage the Temple Mount; standing guard at the entrances and exits and the Israeli police work closely with the Islamic Waqf to provide safe entrance at the specific times during the day for non-Muslims to tour the Temple Mount. The Islamic world needs to understand that the Israeli authority upholds and defends Al-Aqsa Mosque and the status quo by actively restricting Jews, religious or otherwise, who enter it because it is the country (Israel) law which must be abide by the agreement of the status quo of this holy site.[4]

Furthermore, one must consider that the status quo of the holy sites has nothing to do with Islam. It is a purely political demand of Jordan and agreement with Israel to keep calm in the region. Islam itself has never prohibited Jews from prayer on the Temple Mount; I have not found a single verse of the Quran which prohibits Jews from praying near or inside the Temple Mount, nor any saying of Prophet Muhammad (PBUH) which justifies the current restrictions to maintain the status quo of the holy sites. A 13th-century claim to an extended region of holiness was made by Ibn Taymiyyah (an Islamic Scholar), who asserted: "Al-Masjid al-Aqsa is the name for the whole of the place of worship built by Solomon (known as Solomon's Temple)."[5]

We Muslims have been ordered by the Prophet (Peace Be Upon Him) to visit three mosques; Masjid-al-Haram (House of Allah in Makkah – or Mecca), Masjid-e-Nabvi (Mosque of Prophet – PBUH in Madinah) and Masjid-e-al Quds (Al-Aqsa mosque), if

---

4 https://www.adl.org/education/resources/backgrounders/jerusalem-and-the-temple-mount-status-quo

5 The Rise of Jihadist in the West, Chapter 2, page 21

we can afford to do so. It is not obligatory upon Muslims to visit Al-Quds mosque (Harm-e-Sharif). The Al - Aqsa Mosque was the first house of God to Muslims, but then it was changed by Allah to Makkah. Now we have no Islamic obligation to pray towards Jerusalem, therefore we cannot claim Al-Aqsa as part of Islamic ritual; however, it is the most sacred place for Muslims *after* two grand Mosques (in Makkah and Medina). (For a few years in the early stages of Islam, Muhammad, Peace Be Upon Him, instructed his followers to face the Mount during prayer which changed to Makkah afterwards.)

The issue of Al-Aqsa mosque is now more a political objective than a religious ritual in that the Palestinian political leadership uses this holy place for their own political objectives; the status quo is more useful for propaganda and incitement purposes rather than any religious requirement or respect. A fundamental principle of Islam is that the life of a human being, be it Jew or Muslim, is more sacred than the Al-Aqsa mosque. Allah made no distinction between the life of a Muslim and a non-Muslim. Life may only be taken as a means of self-defence in a just war. By devising an imaginary threat to the status quo of Al-Aqsa mosque, Palestinians attempt to incite an imaginary "just war" and provoke their manipulated call for Muslims to trigger a reflex of "self-defence" where there is no threat, no war and no need to defend.

From my understanding, the status quo of this and other holy sites has no religious foundation whatsoever, and therefore I completely rule out this agreement. I believe that Jews possess the same rights to worship on the Temple Mount as we Muslims have to worship in the house of Allah in Makkah (Kingdom of Saudi Arabia). I do not feel uncomfortable in saying that a revised status quo must be established to grant the Jews permission to pray to the same one true God, HaShem, as we do without fear of any persecution. Islam is a religion of peace, and it seeks to obtain peace, but unfortunately, Muslim radicals, especially Arabs, manipulate the origin of Islam to pursue their own political agendas and goals. In the Quran, Allah said: And if they incline to

72

peace, incline you also to it......[6]

Israel and Israeli citizens want peace, but their offers of peace have always been rejected by so-called Palestinians and some other political Arab Muslims. In essence, they aren't simply turning away from the peace offered by Israel, but they are actually rejecting the message of peace offered by Allah in the light of above-mentioned Quranic verse.

Islam prohibits strikes against any regime that has granted the Islamic religious rights to their citizens, and there are some 400 mosques in Israel under the protection of Israeli law and government, including the Al-Aqsa Mosque. Muslims inside and outside Israel have absolutely no religious justification to lash out at the State of Israel by whatever means. Israel's 1.7 million Muslim and Christian Arab citizens make up 20% of her overall population. [7] They enjoy the same social and political rights and freedoms as every other Israeli citizen and, for the majority, are as committed and faithful to the state of Israel as their Jewish citizens.

Islam never taught its followers to hate Jews. There are many Quranic verses which praised Jewish people as the children of Israel, and we must understand the reality that this nation is a peaceful nation in the world. Israel is the country which always welcomes people from around the world and is in the forefront of offering and delivering help and aid to any other country and or peoples of any religion and nationality. Israel is the holy land, the blessed land of the prophets of the three Western religions, and it must remain a peaceful land in the world.

The Muslim attitude towards Israel is based on lies, bias and hate. This is simply hypocrisy, bigotry and abysmal ignorance. We Muslims must change our position towards the State of Israel and the Jewish people because not only does it disrespect the real image of Israel and her people, but it also projects a negative and

---

6   The Holy Quran: 08:61

7   http://mfa.gov.il/MFA/ForeignPolicy/Issues/Pages/Facts-and-Figures-Is-lam-in-Israel.aspx

intolerant image of Muslims.

There is no difference between anti-Zionism and anti-Semitism; both acts are against the Jewish nation their right to a Jewish State regardless of political affiliation. The name of the Jews is used as the symbol of hate in the Islamic world. The Jewish identity is enough to be detested. This Muslim behaviour must be condemned because it is not a message of Islam.

The Prophet of Islam married to two Jewish women at different times (who embraced Islam afterwards by their own wish) to hold strong relations with his cousins. This is the tangible example of coexistence of the Prophet Muhammad (PBUH) towards Jews. We must abide by our cousins (Jews) with love and peace. They hold full right to pray in the Mount Temple as we have because they pray to the same and one true God as we do. The Jewish nation is the first monotheistic nation of the universe and we (Muslims) came after them.

The Israel-Palestine Conflict and Iran's role of Interest

The Middle East is important to the West both economically and strategically, and the prospect of a number of these states being ruled by political leaders in the name of Islam or the idea that these states might actually be ruled by the clerical establishment is alarming. In the late 1930s, modernist Islamist figures such as Hassan al-Banna recognised the symbolic importance of the unfolding conflict between Jews and Arabs in Palestine.

Long before the creation of Israel in 1948, or even after, the war between the Jews and the Arabs started in and around Jerusalem. Jerusalem or al-Quds (The holy) as it is known in Arabic, assumes deep importance to the Muslim faithful including the Islamists. It is a common motif for Muslims. Religious issues around this conflict turned into political terrorism, political figures of Palestine and some radical Islamists ignite this matter for their political and religious cause. Terrorism is the main threat the world currently faces. Terrorism has some strong national and transnational support; people find confusion in the phenomenon of resistance, insurgency, freedom fighting and Terrorism.

To kill civilians for political achievement is terrorism. Freedom fighters or insurgents do not kill civilians, they only target military installations and governmental infrastructures to destabilise the state. From my understanding, the state of Israel is facing two types of regional terrorism with the assistance of cross border outfits.

- Political terrorism

- Religious terrorism

There are two mainstreams political cum nationalist and religious organisations that have countered Israel for over last 5 decades. Fattah, in back dated, a Palestinian Liberation Organisation (PLO), which is a political cum nationalist organisation and Hamas as Islamic resistance Movement which is a political cum religious organisation. Fattah uses a political tool to achieve a religious goal and Hamas uses a religious tool to achieve a political end but both organisation's common agenda and objective is to create chaos within the boundaries of Israel and to destabilise the state politically and economically, though both organisations are apparently opposed to each other but their dangerous goal towards the Israel remains same.

Fattah (PA) and Hamas are the two main powers of Palestinian politics. They hijacked the cause of Palestine and Palestinians for their political violence-based agenda. There are around 2 million Muslims live in Israel, but their family members/relatives/ friends are residing in Gaza and the West Bank respectively. Fatah and Hamas do not want their people to live in peace and freedom; they maintain their political power through Palestinian blood. This is the key to their wealth; the blood of their own people is more precious and important than any other Muslim's in the world.

The land of Israel was referred to as the land of blessing but now it has become the land of blood where blood is more crucial than the holy land. Palestinian blood generates money and revenue of Gaza and the West bank, where the political regime plays a bloody game to shed the blood of their people in the name of so-called liberation and freedom. These areas were and are always in political and religious conflict; they are horrific war zones where every single person is at risk of his or her life.

Hate and violence has been induced in people's minds, revenge has become an ideology and racism is their motto, people learn and teach martyrdom in schools, mosques and in Madrasahs. Terrorism is their heroism; terrorists are their future role models. They have no choice but to fulfil their political mission by physically destroying others' lives and economically destabilise the victim's country.

Their life is valueless, their future is dark and their civilian administrative infrastructure is completely damaged. The Palestinian people suffer from their corruption, cruelty and states inflation. [8]In fact, the Palestinians are victims more of their political and religious leaders than at the Israeli reaction. Their political leaders persistently compel Palestinians to elect them and they have been inflicted over them for years and years.

These political organisations receive huge money not only from Israel but also from all around the world through aids and charities. They are supposed to strengthen their economy to change their people's lifestyle, to stabilise civilian administrative infrastructure and to maintain better and strong relations with the rest of the world, but instead they propagate hate and violence, they advertise their despicable motto through the Palestinian media. Hamas and Fattah deliberately sacrifice their people, and they raise their kids to commit suicide, and they use their children as human shield in war with Israel. They are real blood mongers and blood suckers.

How could they build their own state as their hands are shaded with the blood of their own innocent people! A state cannot be built on blood, hate, violence and revenge. Peace is the only solution which could wash blood shaded hands with love.

Hamas a Sunni radical group, has very close ties with the Shia majority country, Iran. Iran uses Hamas for its political benefits,

---

8   https://tradingeconomics.com/palestine/corruption-index

when Hamas emerged; Iran did not show an interest in Hamas being a Sunni organisation but they did show an interest in Hezbollah being a Shia terrorist organisation. There were three eras or stages between Iran and Hamas to maintain their political mutual relations against the state of Israel.

Stages 1- In the late 1980s, relations between the two were only marginal, principally because Iran's attention was focused elsewhere. Iran's interests were in mobilising Shiites in the Gulf, in supporting international terror, and in building up Hezbollah with a sectarian-flavoured radicalism. These actions grated on Hamas – a radical Sunni movement. Hamas also viewed Iranian support for the Jihad al-Islamic, a different Palestinian faction, as a threat to its standing in the domestic Palestinian arena.

Stage 2- The second stage began with the invasion of Iraq in 1991 and its subsequent containment. Though US policy spoke of dual containment, the containment policy was imposed far more harshly on Iraq. Iran began to view itself as a potential regional hegemony, if not the leader of the Third World. It was the only regional power that was endowed with both a large population and plentiful natural resources. Even Turkey could not compete with that combination at a time when Egypt, the regional power in the 1960s and 1970s and Iran's natural foe, continued its relative decline under Mubarak. Iran began focusing on increasing state power and control over states guided by radical and fanatical conviction.

Stage 3- During this period (1993 to 2000), Hamas also suffered from limited public support. Palestinian pollsters consistently found that a mere 14-18 percent of the respondents supported Hamas, while double the percentage of respondents supported Fattah. For this reason, Hamas refrained from participating in the Palestinian elections of 1996.

Iran found it far more worthwhile to invest in Hezbollah, located in the post-Taif agreement Lebanon, rather than Hamas.[9] If it

---

9   http://carnegieendowment.org/2016/05/16/unraveling-of-lebanon-s-taif-agreement-limits-of-sect-based-power-sharing-pub-63571

adroitly played its cards right, Iran could possibly dominate a state bordering Israel. Hamas is an offshoot of the Muslim Brotherhood (Ikhwan-ul-Muslimoon) in Gaza, MB of Egypt appointed slain Sheikh Ahmed Yasin as its Palestinian branch head, who not only successfully led the organisation but made a charter of Hamas as well; Sheikh Yasin was very powerful, charismatic and spiritual leader of Hamas. Yasin was a very strong old man, he was arrested by IDF many times and did not disclose anything in the investigation, but his son's screaming during torture in IDF interrogation cell broke Yasin up and he then disclosed hidden ties, cooperation, training method and operational palling with Iran against Israel.

The coming to power of Mohammed Morsi and the Muslim Brotherhood in Egypt in 2012 appeared to represent a significant strategic breakthrough for Hamas.

At the very time that the organisation was pivoting away from Iran, on account of Tehran's activities in the Syrian Civil War, Hamas in Gaza had now acquired a powerful friend on its immediate border. With the Muslim Brotherhood in Egypt being ideologically sympathetic to Hamas' wider goals, this period represented a significant opportunity for rearmament and weapons smuggling. Similarly, the Morsi government proved a useful ally for Hamas when it came to negotiating a ceasefire with Israel during the November 2012 conflict in Gaza.[10]

With Morsi's fall from power in July 2013, however, Hamas not only lost a crucial source of support, but the organization now has to confront the reality of a formidable opponent in the form of President Sisi's administration. The present Egyptian government is not only at odds with Hamas over its association with the now ousted Muslim Brotherhood, but also on account of Cairo's belief that Hamas in Gaza is providing material assistance to jihadist militants in the Sinai. Indeed, as fighting between the Egyptian military and Islamists in the Sinai has intensified, so the policies of Sisi's government have hardened against Hamas. Israel offered a separate state to Palestinian regimes many times but every

---

10 Ibid

time, it was rejected and demanded again whenever the conflict started. Fatah wants its own state and Hamas want its own state, both regimes do not accept power in sharing as it was resulted after the 2006 election when Hamas gained political control of the Palestine region.

Currently, there are already two separate states administrating in Palestine, the administrative government of Gaza run by Hamas and the administrative government in the West bank run by the PA. Both political powers are unable to accept and respect their regional boundaries and yet demand a separate state. This means that the two separate states are run by both political powers separately.

Palestinians can only retain peace in the region, if they overthrow both political and religious regimes of Gaza and the west bank. They can replace a separate political power which would not only maintain real peace with Israel but also protect its jurisdiction and care for the people who are living within its boundaries.

HAMAS: Islamic or a Kharijit Movement

In the last few years of my discussions with pro-Palestinian Muslims who support Hamas, they knowingly or unknowingly don't understand that Hamas does not represent Islam at all because of its un-Islamic terror activities. In this article, I will highlight from the Islamic perspective, that Hamas is not only involved in non-Islamic actions but has its affiliations with Kharijit (extremist renegades).

Here are some un-Islamic activities of Hamas: [11]

1. Murdering innocent people

2. Terrorist activities against civilian

3. Abducting innocent people

4. Corruption and fraud

5. Using women and children as human shields

---

11   https://www.counterextremism.com/threat/hamas

The above listed are the main terrorist objectives which Hamas uses to achieve political ends. People might know that Hamas is an offshoot of the Muslim Brotherhood (Ikhwan ul-Muslimoon) of Egypt. Hamas was born in 1987 just after the first Intifada (Uprising) by Sheikh Ahmed Yassin (at one time was my hero). Hamas is a branch of the Palestine Muslim brotherhood in Gaza and the West Bank. Before you understand Hamas, you must understand the ideology of the Muslim Brotherhood. Before you understand the ideology of the Muslim Brotherhood, you must understand the Juhayman movement which hijacked the Ka'abah (House of Allah in Saudi Arabia) in 1979 which was then blamed for Iran. However, it was actually carried out by the Juhayman movement, the people within Saudi Arabia, along with students of Ka'abah-Makkah.

Juhayman movement was a Kharijit (extremist renegades) movement headed by Juhayman Al-Utaybi. There were many Juhayman's who escaped from the Operation and or released from the Saudi prisons decades later. They sought refuge in Pakistan, India and Egypt and joined different extremist organisations. In Pakistan, one of their renounce religious leaders then created an organisation which now is called Jamat-ul-Dawah (LeT), a world proclaimed declared a terrorist organisation. In Egypt, they joined the Muslim Brotherhood. Juhayman himself, with his followers were beheaded in Saudi Arabia, but Juhayman's influence remained alive in the world. One of the pilgrims who had watched the takeover in Mecca had taken a Juhayman leaflet (small booklet) home with him to Egypt. YaroslavTrofimov, an author of the book, "The Siege of Makkah" describes him as sharing it with exciting tales of the Mecca events with his brother Khaled, a first lieutenant in the Egyptian army, who began an eighteen month "path to martyrdom." [12]

It would be this brother, in 1981, which would fire several bullets into the "Pharaoh" Anwar Sadat, Egypt's president, for making peace with the Jews.

One of those who had a "personal bond" with Juhayman's

---

12 The Siege of Makkah, Chapter 3, page 31

movement was a Palestinian preacher, Isam al Barqawi, otherwise known as Abu Mohammed al Maqdisi. He wrote that Juhayman had been wrong about the Mahdi but that this was, "nothing compared to the enormous crimes of the Saudi government." [13] He argued that by sending soldiers against Juhayman, the Saudi state was the first to violate Quranic prohibitions against waging warfare in "the holy precinct." Trofimov writes that one of those influenced by Maqdisi was the person who planted the bomb, in November 1995 that destroyed the National Guard building in Riyadh killing seven people, including five Americans. Maqdisi at this time was behind bars in Jordan. His cell mate, "a co-conspirator and favoured pupil," was Abu Musab al Zarqawi, the future leader of al Qaeda in Iraq.

Juhayman had close ties with Egypt's Muslim brotherhood and Hamas is an offshoot of the Ikhwan movement in Egypt. The influence of Juhayman ideology remained strong within the Ikhwan movement which was then passed to Palestinian's Hamas movement. These movements are against the Saudi Arabian monarchy system. This is why KSA (Kingdom of Saudi Arabia) did not intend to support the Muslim brotherhood and Hamas while Iran always did.

One of the Hamas's main terror tactics is to launch suicide attacks against the Israeli civilians which are completely against the teachings of Islam.

The grand mufti of Saudi Arabia, Sheikh Abd al-Aziz bin Abdallah Aal al-Sheikh, said in 2001, that "Islam forbids suicide terrorist attacks".[14] Ikhwan movement (Muslim brotherhood) which was deeply rooted in Al-Azhar University of Egypt, were taught in this religious institute. Many Al-Azhar scholars and even Muftis of Egypt were anti-Semitic with their speeches and fatwas against Israelis. They defended Hamas' suicide terrorism against the Jewish state of Israel.

---

13 Call for Transnational Jihad, Chapter 1, page 34

14 http://www.washingtoninstitute.org/policy-analysis/view/the-saudi-fat-wa-against-suicide-terrorism

On one hand Saudi's grand mufti issued a fatwa against suicide terrorism and on the other hand Al-Azhar (Egypt) mufti issued a fatwa in favour of Hamas' suicide terrorism.[15] This fatwa clearly indicated that Hamas was a direct religious and political cult of the Ikhwan. The fatwa of Egypt's mufti was a challenge of the KSA (Kingdom of Saudi Arabia) religious block. Shaykh Ali Abu al-Hasan, chairman of the committee of rulings in al-Azhar, stated, "fighting the enemy with any kind of defence is a duty." He called the Palestinians to, "go on hitting Jewish targets and bring an earthquake under the feet of the traitors, the people of the virus state."The general argument of various Islamist groups or individuals has been that, "all means are legitimate to fight the Jews," as argued by Sheikh Sayyid Wafa, secretary-general of the Islamic research centres of al-Azhar in Egypt.

I see these Egyptian fatwas and their religious opinions different than the teachings of Islam. Allah says in the Quran: "... if someone kills another person – unless it is in retaliation for someone else or for causing corruption in the earth – it is as if he had murdered all mankind. And if anyone gives life to another person, it is as if he had given life to all mankind. ..." This is the same message mentioned in the holy book of Torah.[16]

Hamas kills innocent civilians and Al-Azhar, Egypt's Islamic religious authority, defends Hamas' killing and its bombing of people, which I see as un-Islamic acts according to the above verse of the holy Quran.

Allah/HaShem is most merciful to mankind. Why it is the Palestinian followers of Hamas became more ruthless and yet they claim that they are the true followers of Islam, even though they kill other people under the name of Islam? Allah says in Quran: "... God is All-Gentle, Most Merciful to mankind." They have manipulated the true meaning of Jihad by killing innocent

---

15   https://www.brookings.edu/articles/must-innocents-die-the-islamic-de-
    bate-over-suicide-attacks/

16   The Babylonian Talmud, Translated by Michael L. Rodkinson – Book 8: Sec-
    tion Jurisprudence (Damages), [Bostin, The Talmud Society, 1918] – Tract
    Sanhedrin, page 1747

souls in the world. "Waging jihad" in Islam means to educate the other side, to teach moral virtue and to raise awareness to turn people away from evil. Those who murder in the name of jihad are not acting in the light of the Qur'an.

Islam never promoted slaughtering Jews but sheltered them when they needed. The Quranic rulings on wars and on general prospects are far different in reality. Some ignorant people and organisations such as Al-Qaeda, Taliban, ISIS, Hamas, Hezbollah and others manipulate the Quranic rulings of war positions and place them on the current general situation which is pure ignorance and nothing else. These organisations and their followers act against the teachings of Allah.

Allah does not like corruption on earth, and killing innocents and creating chaos within civilian population is a great corruption on earth. Allah says in the holy Quran: **"Allah does not love corruption"**.[17]

The people who support Hamas have forgotten the teachings and ruling of the holy Quran. In Islam, even in wars you have to show mercy towards non-combatant civilians. The Prophet of Islam, Muhammad (PBUH), sets some rules and regulation of wars, in which the Islamic army cannot kill innocents, women, elders, children, non-combatants and no military can destroy marketplaces, business and even worship places I ask the question for those who think that Hamas is fighting an Islamic war against Jews and Israel. Can you justify Hamas attacks, according to the Islamic teachings which I mentioned above in the Islamic rules and regulations of wars? Can you justify killing women, children, elders, mutilating them through suicide terrorism in Israel? Can you justify destroying their places of worships, markets and business places by bombing them?

Hamas is not an Islamic organisation but a Kharijit (extremist renegades) by carrying out un-Islamic teachings within its jurisdiction (Gaza). They do not represent the true, peaceful and merciful message of Islam towards non-Muslims, especially to

---

17   The Holy Quran: 2:205

Jews. Hamas abducts people, torture and execute their political prisoners, kills innocent women, children and elders. They create mischief on earth, steal lands, involved in corruption, and use their own children and women as human shields. We cannot call them freedom fighters, Muslim defenders or the followers of Islam. They are Ikhwan's ideological ruthless cult and Juhayman (Kharijities) followers who attacked Ka'abah, the house of Allah in Makkah. If you still think what Hamas does is an Islamic act and they are following the true Islamic teachings, then you are the most ignorant people on earth and I am free from your Islam. I would not follow the Islam that teaches us to kill innocent people, destroy their cities and to commit terrorist acts to achieve political ends. We must follow the real teachings of Islam, which teaches us to love our enemy, treat others with kindness and establish a peaceful environment in the world in that the followers of other religions live safe and secure with harmony.

The holy Quran says: "Surely those who believe, and those who are Jews, and the Christians and the Sabians, whoever believes in God and the Last Day, and does good, they have their reward with their Lord, and there is no fear for them, nor shall they grieve."[18]

The Arab Nationalism, Islamism and the State of Israel

Arab nationalism is entirely different from Islam. Islamic ideology is humanistic while Arab nationalism does not preserve Islam. Turkey is affixed to socialist Ataturk and Egypt with Gamal Abdel Nasser. All Muslims are not against Israel, but some Arab states do not tolerate a modern country like Israel in the region. Since the creation of the Jewish state of Israel in 1948, the attitude of the Arab Kings has been hostile towards Israel because they were scared of the newly established Jewish state. They knew the Jewish state was more capable than the rest of the Arab states. They could not surpass the state in every field of life, from technology to military capability.

The bloody history of the Arab's barbarism is full of genocide. Arabs did not desire a potent non-Arab country within their

---

18 The Holy Quran: 2:62

neighbourhood. Therefore, they tried hard to destabilise the Jewish nation by attacking them. Jordan, Syria, Lebanon and Egypt were ruled by nationalist arrogant Arab leaders who advocated socialism for decades. The six day-Ramadan-war (1967) was initiated by the Arab nationalist leaders. They lost their war because this war was not an Islamic war, but an Arab nationalist war against the lone Jewish nation which was a heavy threat to them and their cruel regimes.

There are 10 out of 56 Islamic nations in the world who have recognised Israel. Turkey was the first Islamic country who recognised Israel. Iran recognized Israel in 1952 but adopted a hostile attitude towards the Jewish state. While there have been 15 wars between Israel and the Arabs and Palestinians, in every war, the Arabs were defeated. There are many reasons behind their humiliating defeat and one of them is their socialistic and nationalistic ideology which contradicted with their religion.

The Arab states have nothing to do with Islam, but they pride themselves to be Arabs instead of being Muslims. The Arab Israeli wars were not based on religious ideology, but for the greed of land. That is why, when the Six Day War started, Egyptian leader Anwar al Sadat delivered his speech in which he stated, "Oh descendants of the Pharaohs! You are contending with the sons of the Moses who had defeated us ages ago; now it's time for you to call for revenge."[19]

The Arab nationalism had hijacked Islam, adopted a Takfiri ideological thought, and manipulated the teachings of Islam to be used against the Jewish community. As exhibited by the Egyptian leader Anwar al Sadat, they pride themselves in being descendants of Pharaohs rather than Muslims. Additional grounds for their defeat were that the resources of their military power were negligible. Whenever Saudi Arabia experiences trouble within the land, they seek help from Pakistan to protect them. One example was during the Arab spring in Bahrain. The Pakistan Army in the uniform of the Saudi Army entered into Bahrain and completely halted the uprising. When the Arab-Israeli Six Day War started;

---

19 *Arutz Sheva News*, THE REAL STORY: An inevitable conflict - The Six-Day War, 2nd June 2017

the Pakistani army participated in the warfare against the Israel, though Israel never did so with Pakistan.

The Arabs leaders always supported terrorism to damage the Israel's governmental and civilian infrastructure. They fought many wars, but were defeated in every measure of war against the Jewish state. They also destroyed Afghanistan, Pakistan, Iraq and Syria by providing arms and funds to the terrorist organizations in the region. There is no democracy or freedom of speech and human rights for their public. Israel is the only country in the Middle East with a great democratic rule and freedom of speech and equal rights for minorities.

Arabs can never accept a Jewish state near their borders because of the historical and sectarian background which prohibits them to support the Jewish people or Zionism. Terrorism is the weapon of these Arab nationalists. They stand and promote terrorism not only against the State of Israel, but against non-Arab Muslim states as well. After wars with Israel and defeat, they realised that they cannot gain ground in the war against Israel. Therefore, they created terrorist groups against Israel to shake every city of it with the flame of terrorism. Arab nationalists have another great danger within their borders, which is an Islamic violent extremism. They tried hard to defeat this ideology, but could not succeed. They lost their political leaders and head of states to Islamists. In fact, Israel never was a danger to an Arab country, nonetheless Arab countries attacked Israel. Arabs perceive that Zionist leaders as their utmost hope to survive so they eventually will normalise their relations with Zionists against Islamists.

For Arabs, Zionists are the actual problem of all matters they cannot solve. Jews never were a problem for Muslim states before the 19th century. Many Muslim states had good relations with Jews anywhere from businesses to the governments and the Jews always supported them. They didn't want to see a solid and powerful Jew who can talk to them loudly for their rights and exemption. The root of the conflict lay then at the end of the nineteenth century in ethno-political rather than purely religious differences. Under the rule of the Ottoman Turks; the Jews,

Christians and Muslims of Palestine coexisted peacefully under the framework of Islamic governance.

The relationship between Arabs and Jews heated up when Theodore Herzl published his treaties in 1896. He argued that assimilation of the Jews would never happen and that the Jews should find their own state, preferably in Palestine. The Zionist movement was not different than Judaism because it aspired Judaism, but the difference was only that Judaism was based on religious actions. However, Zionism was based on both political action and destiny. A Sudanese theologian stated: "Judaism is a religion in which the believers follow a certain creed. Zionism is the same as Judaism, but it seeks to achieve the end sought by Judaism but through political actions."[20]

Arabs, however, consider Zionism as entirely different as Judaism because they were habituated to living with Jews who were dwelling in fear under their dominion. However, Zionism was a powerful movement with a group of strong Jews who desired a separate state for their people where they can become robust. This was the only reason that Arabs did not want a Jewish state. The Arab nationalism is also opposed to Islam and this is why Islamists were always in battle with Arab nationalists. However, at the same time, Islamists were against Zionists because of the ideology of political Islam, which contradicted with the political philosophy of Zionism.

Arab leaders, especially Egyptian political leaders, were not Muslims, but socialists and they were not happy to see Islamists rise up against their regimes. The modern Islamist figures such as Hasan al-Banna recognised the symbolic importance of the unfolding conflict between Jews and Arabs in Palestine. He is quoted as criticising Egyptian nationalists with regard to the issue: "Political bodies as parties in Egypt were totally diverted from supporting Palestine seriously because their nationalism had not reached the stage of developing a feeling for Arabism and

---

20 Jerusalemonline, 16 May 2016

for the Islamic bond."[21]

Arab Nationalist political leaders would never end their conflict with Israel, even if Israel conceded the entire West Bank and Jerusalem because they perceive every single Jew as the main problem for all Arab nationalists. They will not cease their conflict against Israel until one inch of Palestine is occupied by no Zionists. One former Israeli colonel asserted: "On the contrary it may encourage them to say that a withdrawal to [the 1967 border] is just the beginning of the Salah a-Din victory on the heretics."

We Pakistanis have not any issue with Israel or Zionism but we only blindly supported the Palestinian cause for money and pressure from the Arab nationalist leaders. Whenever India attacked Pakistan, these Palestinian leaders never helped and supported the Islamic state of Pakistan. PLO leader Yasser Arafat was a close friend of Indian leaders and he always considered Indira Gandhi (Slain Prime Minister of India) as his elder sister and we not only nurtured them, but provided them financial, civilian and military support against the State of Israel.

This is not a war of Islam or a war of Non-Arabs, but a war of Arab nationalists. Muslims should not suffer any fear and danger from the State of Israel. Yet, Arabs used Islam and promoted Political cum Religious Jihad against Jews and Israel to fulfil their dirty and greedy political desires. We must understand who and what to follow because Arab ideology is not an Islamic ideology but a socialist political theory.

---

21 Ibid

CHAPTER 5

THE HEAT WITHIN THE STATE OF ISRAEL

Burning Intifada, the Arab Israelis and the Islamic Ruling

Several days ago, there was a disaster in the city of Haifa in Israel when heavy fires flared and spread across and covered neighbouring cities as well. The state of Israel sought help from the western countries, including Turkey and Russia. The fires were under investigation and it was confirmed later that the fires were not caused from natural disaster, but from an act of arson which was committed by some extremist Arab Israelis. The Palestinian Salafist organisation claimed its responsibility. In the past few days, Muslims, especially in the Arab world, rejoiced on social media and celebrated immensely due to the cause of fire in Haifa. They showed their great happiness and joy. They were chanting and saying, "Israel banned Adhaan so Allah sent fire to Israel" and, "it was Allah's punishment for Jews." "Israel is burning. Israel is in hell fire," they chanted while displaying a joyful atmosphere everywhere.

The accusation of banning Adhaan by the Israeli cabinet was a blame, nothing else. The bill only restricts the excess of Mosques external loudspeakers on certain timings and yet it needs to be approved by the Israeli Parliament (Knesset). It was very devastating that this act of terrorism was committed by some Israeli Muslims (Extremist Arabs) who enjoy their full and equal rights in the Jewish state of Israel. They have every enjoyment of life in Israel as Israeli Jews have. They have no excuse to play with the lives of Jews and other Muslims of Israel.

People are calling this act a Burning Intifada or Burning Jihad against the state of Israel and peaceful Muslims must condemn this because this terror attempt damaged innocent peoples' quality of life and property. Thousands of people (Muslims and Jews) were dispersed from their homes. These acts are not permitted according to the teaching of Islam. Islam never allows their people to harm any human without a certain legal procedure (punishment) of the law of the country.

There were many critical situations in the history of the state of Israel, including the Palestinian Intifada, Al-Aqsa Intifada, Stabbing Intifada and now, recently, the Burning Intifada. All of these acts of terrorism are forbidden according to the teachings of the Quran and the Hadith (Sayings of the Prophet of Islam PBUH). There is no religious justification to carry out these types of terror activities in the name of Allah Almighty and Islam forbids the killing of an innocent human.

Peace is the main motto of Islam and the religion of Islam stands with the pillar of Peace. The Arabic word "Imaan" which means, "Belief" in English, has a very important role in a Muslim's faith. We cannot be Muslims if we do not have a belief (Imaan) in certain Islamic pillars. The word "Imaan" came from the Arabic word, "Aman" which means, "Peace" the other Arabic related word is "Amanah" which means, "Trust or Honesty." The word, "Ameen" means the one who is honest and trustworthy in English. So, all these other words such as "Aman" (Peace), "Amanah" (Trust, Honest) and "Ameen" (trustworthy) are directly related with the word "Imaan" (Belief). If any of the word is missing in Muslim's practical life, he/she has no "Imaan" belief or faith anymore.[1]

Muslims must be peaceful and "Ameen" (Honest and trustworthy) towards others and we must provide an "Aman" (safety and security) to other religions and nations. Without these basic principles of "Imaan" (belief), we no longer are able

---

1   The Rise of Jihadist Extremism in the West, Introduction, page 7

to call ourselves Muslims. A Muslim must have to be honest with everyone, speak truth, even if truth goes against him anyway. Muslims should not lie even about enemies and must not spread lies based on propaganda. In the teaching of Islam and according to the Quran, "if a non-believer brings news, which is based on true content, Muslims must accept it." Muslims cannot reject the most accurate news for the reason that it belongs to non-Muslims. This is not a teaching of Islam. How can Muslims spread lies and propaganda against the people (Jews) who believe in one true God and even can eat their Halal/Kosher food?

The neighbour holds a special status in Islam. Islam encourages Muslims to treat their neighbours in a gentle way that reflects the true and genuine spirit of Islam as exemplified in its tolerant aspect--especially with people of other faiths (Jews and Christians). According to the teachings of Islam, our neighbour is not who live next door to our home only. Neighbour is inclusive of those we work with, shop, eat, and do business with, those we walk through the streets with, including anyone who lives in our town. Good Muslim should not wrong his neighbour with regard to his physical wellbeing, his wealth or his honour. A true Muslim should not transgress against neighbours' wealth by stealing, betraying or deceiving, and he should not harm him physically by striking or killing him.

The Prophet of Islam (PBUH) instructed that individuals will not enter into Jannah (Paradise) if the neighbour is not happy with him through his actions. In another saying of the Prophet (PBUH) is that the person is not a Muslim if he harms his neighbour by any means. The Prophet of Islam said: "He will not enter Paradise whose neighbour is notsecure from his evil."[2]These instructions are for everyone regardless of his religion (people of books and Pagans).

I would like to ask those that do harm, how they call themselves Muslims, even though they kill innocent people, harm their neighbours and create mischievousness on the land where

---

2   http://www.askourimam.com/2016/02/01/tolerance-in-islam

they live and were born? The Jewish people living in Israel are neighbours of those Muslims (Palestinian Arabs) who are Israeli citizens or of those living in the West Bank or in Gaza. They have absolutely no right to harm innocent people in any way. If they do so, according to the instructions of the Prophet of Islam (PBUH), "they are no more Muslims." [3]

Palestinian Muslims cannot raise their arms against the state of Israel due to a few reasons.

1. Israel is a Jewish state (people of the book)

2. Muslims in the state are not under religious persecution

3. The religion of Islam and the places of worship (Mosques) are legally protected by the state

4. The state of Israel provides safety and security to them and their places of worship

Those Israeli Arabs who aren't following the democratic laws of the state are not peaceful Muslims but oppressors. If they create mischief in the holy land of Israel, they are no more believers according the teachings of Islam. There is no difference between Muslims living under the rules of Christians in the UK or under the rules of Jews in Israel because both countries have democratic governments and have been given full legal rights as their citizens, including freedom of speech, freedom of movement, freedom to exercise their religion, freedom of living equally and the basic human rights without a fear of persecution.

Those Muslims who burned the forest and burnt thousands of living trees are lawfully accountable to the justice of the state of Israel as well as to Allah the Almighty hereafter. The crime of burning living trees is as equivalent as burning humans alive because it is a great punishment in Islam for burning living trees. Fear Allah, as you will be judged according to your actions, not according to your belief. If you aren't a good human, you cannot be a good Muslim. You cannot seek Jannah (paradise) until you

---

3   http://opinion.premiumtimesng.com/2015/05/29/the-neighbours-rights-in-islam-by-imam-murtada-gusau

are a good neighbour, peaceful, trustworthy, harmless and law-abiding citizen and until the people around you are safe from your evil. The Prophet of Islam (PBUH) said: "A Muslim is, who stays in one of the mountain paths worshipping Allah and leaving the people secure from his mischief."[4]

Is Muezzin Bill a Religious Discrimination in Israel

A few weeks ago, Israeli Cabinet Ministers passed a bill in which they suggested to ban using the loudspeaker during the Adhaan (a Muslim call to prayer) time. Muslims all around the world are criticising the Israeli government for its anti-religious law which they believe to be an act of direct discrimination against Muslims living in Israel. Israel did not ban Adhaan but restricted the volume of Adhaan by using loudspeakers. This bill has not been presented in the Israeli Parliament (Knesset) yet, and it can be challenged in the high court before or after passing. Some Muslims or human rights' organisations are considering a legal fight, preventing this bill from becoming a law in Israel. My attention has been drawn to this consideration by pro-Israel and anti-Israel Muslims supporters and people were expecting to hear my views as a Muslim Zionist and strong supporter of Israel. I can no longer be silent and, although I am not an Israeli government spokesperson, Muslims from my community need my point of view on this burning issue.

I have never supported any anti-religious and anti-human rights' laws passed whether by Pakistan, Israel or any Western or Arab countries. I assessed this situation very carefully as to whether it is categorised under the violation of human rights or not. Israel is not a perfect country and neither are their political or governmental policies. However, we must weigh Israel's political policies in comparison to other Islamic countries where they have zero human rights for their minority community whom they consider second-class citizens.

Before we comment or discuss emotionally on this bill, we must evaluate the situation very deeply and examine the area where

---

4 Sahih Bukhari, Chapter 52, verse 45

these Mosques are located. Unfortunately, it is a political matter which has been dragged into a religious one which gains more sympathy. The bill has been submitted by a member of the Israeli Parliament who belongs to a Jewish home, and is a member of the religious right-wing party in coalition with the Likud ruling party. The same bill was introduced by the left-wing labour party government as well, and they only agreed to some clauses of the bill.

This bill was amended and represented in the cabinet and finally was approved by it. The bill was presented again and again due to increasing complaints of local Jewish neighbours.

The consideration of this law did not surprise me at all as living in England where this type of law is already implemented. No person has had any issue following it. Wherever there are non-Muslims living in the area, there must be limited loudspeaker noise. The Islamic teachings are to create a peaceful atmosphere for neighbours during the night or dawn times. In the UK, Muslims are not allowed to open a mosque even in Muslim areas where non-Muslim neighbours do not give permission. Still, we have no problem with the law. Millions of Muslims living in the UK are happily following the rules and regulations of the country, whether it is a political or religious based law.

Mosques in the UK never use external loudspeakers and the same law also implements all across the Europe and in the US as well. The state of Israel is a Jewish state not a Muslim country and same law should be applied there as in any European country.

In protesting against this law, a prominent Israeli Arab member of Parliament (MK), Ayman Odeh, called Azzan in the parliament, [5] and his video had become viral on social media. Hundreds of thousands of Muslims across the world show their support and solidarity to Ayman Odeh. I see his act of delivering Azzan in the Israeli parliament in a positive way. Israeli law is what gives him

---

5   http://www.independent.co.uk/news/world/middle-east/arab-politician-performs-muslim-call-prayer-israeli-parliament-protest-against-law-quieten-mosques-a7424206.html

a legal right to protest in the Israeli parliament (Knesset) which he did successfully. The world will never find these basic human rights of minorities elsewhere in the Muslim world, including the Kingdom of Saudi Arabia, Iran, Iraq, and Syria, Pakistan and in other Arab or non-Arab countries where minorities are heavily suffering from Muslim's persecution.

In Islam, neighbours have more rights and Islam never supports any act which may harm the neighbours anyway. If there exist non-Muslim neighbours, we must respect their basic rights which include the right to sleep in the night time, the right of their pregnant women, the right of their minor children, the rights of their elders, as well as patients. During the day or at night time, people sleep and they do not want to be disturbed. We Muslims must accept their priorities because it is an obligation on Muslims to look after the neighbours' fundamental rights.

I have heard some voices on social media from the Muslim community stating that "Muslims have been living in these areas for a long time and question why the Israeli government needs this ban to be imposed NOW!" If they look at the history, they would find that it is not a new issue but an ongoing issue for decades.

In 1992, this issue has been referred to the Jerusalem Magistrate's court by the local Jewish residents who were feeling disturbed and coping with the excessive use of loudspeakers in mosques for decades. The Jerusalem Magistrate's Court imposed a fine to a Muezzin to lower his Azzan (call for prayers) due to disturbance of local Jewish neighbours. The judge also ordered a mosque to lower their Azzan call (Limitation of Loudspeakers usage). If we look at around at other non-Muslim countries, even within the neighbouring Arab countries, we can find the same issue there where they considered a ban on external loudspeakers in Mosques during the prayer times.

UAE: Dubai Department of Islamic Affairs decided to ban loudspeakers 5 times daily for prayers.

Indonesia: Indonesia's hard-line Islamic Defenders Front (FPI) threw their support behind **calls to curb the excessive use of loud speakers by mosques during Ramadan.** "It is indeed better that mosques adjust their loud speakers when reciting the Koran, so as not to disturb other people." Central Kalimantan's deputy governor, Achmad Diran said: "Don't use loud speakers when reciting the Koran. **Take pity on people of different faiths who want to rest."** [6]

Saudi Arabia: The Ministry of Islamic Affairs banned small mosques from using loudspeakers for the nightly tarawih prayer in Ramadan. "Raising the sound of loudspeakers above the accepted level is not permissible," said Sheikh Tawfiq al-Sayegh, Imam of a mosque in the coastal city of Jeddah, to Okaz daily. "There are ill and elderly people in the neighbouring houses who need rest and quietness."[7]

Egypt: Cairo is said to have 4000 officially recognised mosques that use loudspeakers five times a day and they too have assured noise reduction. [8]

India: the Kerala Samsthana Jamiyathul Ulema, an association of Muslim theologians, has said that there is no need for use of loudspeakers for religious purposes at the mosques and that the Sunni Muslims in Kerala started using the loudspeaker hardly half a century ago. The Delhi High Court on Friday directed all mosques and temples in Ekta Vihar and Sunder Nagri in east Delhi to restrict the decibel level of loudspeakers. It said the loudspeakers should be positioned at a restricted height of only eight feet from the ground. The court also directed them to change the direction of the loudspeakers and make them face the wall of buildings, and not outside, to reduce the noise level.[9]

Sri Lanka: The Supreme Court made a ruling on 9 November 2007 pertaining to loudspeakers. It viewed the right of one party

---

6   Borneo Post Online, 19 July 2012

7   Al-Arabiya News, 29 July 2012

8   http://elderofziyon.blogspot.com/2012/07/muslims-dont-like-loud-calls-to-prayer.html

9   Abid

to use loudspeakers against the annoyance, disturbance and harm caused to other parties who were compelled against their will to listen to the amplified sounds from the loudspeakers. The difference, of course, is when Muslims complain about loud calls to prayer, it is an internal matter. However, when Jews complain, it is Islam phobia.

How do you see the situation in Muslim countries where Jewish synagogues and cemeteries were demolished and turned into theatres, cinemas and shopping centres? Where are the rights of minority communities in Muslim countries? When the Jewish sacred place, Joseph's Tomb site was set ablaze by Palestinian Muslims last year (2015) in West Bank, was their outrage? Why was the Islamic world so silent? What do you think, when the remaining Jewish community is hiding their faith due to Pakistani Muslim's religious persecution against them? Would you call it just and fair under the so-called democratic Law of the country? The Israeli cabinet's approved Muezzin bill, not only addressed the excess of Mosque loudspeakers, but for other religious places, including sounds of Churches as well as Jewish Synagogues. I strongly condemn the criticisms of my Muslim fellows all around the world against this bill, the external speakers of Mosques, and they must be banned completely in the area where they may cause alarm and distress to other religious communities. This represents the teachings of Islam according to the rights of neighbours in the Shariah Law.

Yasser Arafat, A Fake Hero, A Lord of Corruption

The Palestinian Authority (PA) once called the Palestinian Liberation Organization (the PLO). It was chaired by Yasser Arafat, a hero of the Palestinian resistance movement, a godfather of the Palestinian struggle for liberation and an ideological figure for almost every young Palestinian. Very few people knew that Yasser Arafat was a fake hero, a lord of corruption and a true godfather of Palestinian terrorism.

The Palestinian leadership under Yasser Arafat received millions and millions of dollars every year from Western countries and the Muslim world. The Muslim world considered Arafat to be a hero of Jerusalem and even they considered him as a second Saladin, who would finally liberate their land from the Jewish occupation. The Muslim world knew very little or nothing about Yasser's double-faced status. Leaders like him have two faces, two languages, and two sets of promises. When they communicate with the international community, they use one set of languages and values, and make statements and commitments relating to a desire for peace and co-existence. When they turn their faces towards their own nations, they show a monstrous face. When they address their people, they never talk about peace, instead inciting their people towards terrorism. And they are even better at enriching themselves at the expense of the well-being of their people. Yasser Arafat was one of the best of them.

He always used his people to conduct terrorist activities and in return he and his organization received billions of dollars from countries that included Qatar, Iran, Syria, Russia and other Arab countries. Yasser Arafat also never disclosed his actual wealth, even to his party and family. He was one of the most greedy and cruel persons of in the short history of the Palestinians. A friend who worked with Israeli intelligence disclosed that Arafat died along with the knowledge regarding 75% of his secret foreign accounts and no one supposedly knows where they are and how to access them. [10] This is the wealth stolen from Palestinian aid received as donations to change Palestinian lives. The remaining 25% of Arafat's personal accounts were openly transferred to his family. His wife and his daughter live in a most luxurious palace in the Parisian suburbs. Their wealthy life style can be compared to European royalty. According to my Israeli friend, together the two of them spend approximately $50,000 daily maintaining this luxurious and fashionable life style. [11] They even do not bother to live among their own people, people this father and husband supposedly fought a war for during much of his adult life. They care nothing about these people who live in intense poverty, their

---

10 Author's obtained the information from his Israeli friend who worked with Israel's government Intelligence department

11 Abid

only concern is maintaining their lifestyle.

In 2003, The International Monetary Fund (IMF) began to carry out an audit and found at least two billion dollars of Palestinian Authority Fund monies that were missing. [12]It is now believed most probable that these funds were transferred to Arafat's family in Paris. While Yasser Arafat was in a Paris hospital, his wife Soha Arafat agreed to disclose Arafat's medical record on the condition of stopping the ongoing investigation into the missing funds. The PA was very frustrated not to be able to officially locate and recover the missing money which they were assured to have been transferred to Soha Arafat's Swiss bank accounts. Finally, they agreed to pay her $2 million dollars a year for the rest of her life. Whether this means she secretly returned the money or not is speculation.

Israel's Mossad not only believed but provided enough proofs to the government of Israel that Yasser Arafat controlled a personal financial portfolio estimated to be in the region of $6.5 billion. The Arab media, including the Syrian, Jordanian and Lebanese newspapers received a top-secret report regarding the financial status of the PLO, disclosing that for years the PLO had a deficit of over $95 million a month. The report became even more explosive in the Arab world when the IMF revealed that Arafat had diverted a billion dollars or more of PLO funds to his and his and Soha's personal Swiss bank accounts from 1995 to 2000. A Palestinian lawyer who has investigated PLO corruption said, "... [I] knew of four Arafat loyalists who held secret Swiss bank accounts". [13]

The deals frequently involved the cement and building industries of the Palestinian territories. The corruption ran into millions of dollars, which Arafat covered up in return for the profiteers giving him a portion. It was often said Arafat was the godfather of all the godfathers. The secret investments of Yasser Arafat were disclosed by an American financial investigation team and the report stated that Arafat invested his secret money after it

---

12   http://www.adespicabletruce.org.uk/page31.html

13   Gideon's Spies: The secret history of the Mossad, chapter 21, page 441

was transferred from PLO funds to his personal Swiss account. Some of those investments included the Coca Cola bottling plant in Ramallah, a Tunisian cell phone company, and many venture capital funds in the US and the Cayman Islands. The money for a large part of his investment came from public funds like Palestinian taxes. Virtually none of it was used for the welfare of the Palestinian people and it was fully controlled by Arafat and his family. Arafat travelled almost all of the rich Western and Arab countries around the world and crying to everyone that, "We (Palestinians) are devastated and our economy is going to collapse and we cannot pay salaries to Palestinian employees and it is because of Israel's occupation and blockade". [14]

He convinced those countries and the IMF that the words of his mouth were true and if they were not going to fund PLO, the Palestinian economy would be damaged and would collapse completely. They did not yet suspect that Yasser Arafat was draining a huge amount of that money in his personal bank accounts and his people were really still being deprived through high unemployment and poor economy which those funds were supposed to be relieving.

Under the Oslo Accords signed in 1993 and 1995, it was agreed that Israel would collect sales tax on goods purchased by Palestinians living in Israel under Green Card status and transfer that money to Palestinian treasury but instead transferred immediately transferred it into his private accounts. From the outset of the Oslo Accords until 2000, Israel put the tax revenue into Arafat's accounts at Bank Leumi in downtown Tel Aviv. Israel's intent was that Arafat would use it to clean the area of terrorists and for the Palestinians' welfare. According to US officials, Arafat had nearly $3 billion in his personal financial portfolio of the known 25% but, again, this part of his portfolio was already known to the Intelligence departments and the Western financial powers. At that time, nobody was aware of the absconded 75% of the monies, the most part only he-and likely his wife and daughter-knew about.

---

14 Ibid

According to an Israeli official, when Yasser Arafat was alive, he paid $100,000 per month out of the Palestinian budget to his wife Soha who remained in Paris where she lived lavishly on this allowance. Arafat had an additional account in the Swiss bank for the PA but the code name of the account was one only he knew.

There had to have been more than $300 million in his other Swiss account at Bank Lombard Odier,[15] as this is where all the money was transferred to from the Israel's Bank Leumi. As was noted earlier, Arafat's secret Swiss accounts were closed around the time he died and no one will say where that money went.

No one even knows about how high the salary amount was that Arafat collected as a Chairman of PLO when he was in exile. Arafat received hundreds of millions of dollars from the KGB (the USSR's intelligence agency) and the Saudis. The now-deceased Saddam Hussein reportedly handed him a $50,000,000 check for supporting him during the first Gulf war. [16] Where that money gone, I believe Soha Arafat knows. Further scandals where Arafat was directly involved in kickbacks, such as that of the Gas and Petrol's pipeline in Palestinian areas and Arafat's investment in the world's stock markets will be addressed in another article at some point.

Many Palestinian people had and have little money, adequately paying jobs, and own decent homes and businesses. The Arafat's of the Palestinian people have all money to dispense and have everything to fulfill Palestinian dreams. If he could have used that money to push up the Palestinians' economy instead of diverting this money to pay terrorists' salaries, those whose only job is to commit terrorism against the state of Israel, think of what might exist today. He could have built schools and universities that sent Palestinian youngsters, making them an educated person who design new technologies, create medicines, and make the whole world a better place. Instead, he sent them into the training centers in order to create terrorists. Palestinian children

---

15   Ibid

16   Ibid

should be looking at long, healthy, prosperous lives in their own country instead of seeing their only purpose in life as being one to die young.

Yasser Arafat was not a hero of the Palestinians but a mafia lord in a corrupt network. He, his wife and daughter chose to be greedy money mongers who destroyed their people's chance at a real nation and left a dark and hopeless future for the new generation of Palestinian people.

CHAPTER 6

MUSLIM JEWISH HISTORICAL RELATIONS

Muslims Jewish relations, historical conflict and the future for peace[1]

Growing up as a Muslim in Pakistan, I was taught to hate Jews and Israel and to participate in anti-Israel and anti-Zionism demonstrations. Reading into the history of my faith and the history of Islam I came to realise that the perspective adopted by many Muslims today towards Israel and the Jewish people is completely distorted and often deliberately misinformed, for political not religious reasons. While Christianity held historic animosities towards Jews, it was never a phenomenon amongst Muslims. In reality, Muslims frequently supported their Jewish cousins throughout Islamic history.

During the Islamic era in Spain, Jewish people were not only protected, but were free to exercise their beliefs. They held high level government positions in the state of Andalusia. Meanwhile, a virulent form of anti-Semitism afflicted much of Europe. That disease has now, unfortunately, become endemic in the Islamic world. As Europe colonised the Middle East, its anti-Jewish ideas infiltrated the Arab world. We Muslims cannot and should not be anti-Semitic. Our holy book, the Quran supports Judaism. The Prophet of Islam, Muhammad is mentioned only a few times, but the Prophet Moses is mentioned 25 times. In the words of one

---

historian "it was European converts to Islam who brought anti-Semitism into the Arab world."

A new wave of political and religious hatred rose in the 19th century when the Jewish state of Israel emerged. Muslims were told by Europeans, that Jews had taken our holy land and would persecute Muslims, but in fact, this land, especially the city of Jerusalem was a more sacred place to the Jewish people than we Muslims. Muslims were never persecuted under the Jewish state of Israel.

The Jewish state of Israel is a reality now as is the Muslim state of Pakistan. Israel is a land of peace and prosperity where peoples of all faiths live together and exercise their religion without fear of persecution or hate. The state of Israel protects the rights of minorities and their places of worship. The pre-eminent medieval Jewish philosopher and one of the greatest Torah scholars of the middle Ages, served Saladin as his physician in Twelfth century. Jews such as Maimonides became personal physicians of governors in the Islamic era. The most famous example is Samuel Hanagid, who was not only vizier of the Muslim king of Granada, but also a commander of his armies.

It also guarantees freedom of religion for all. Every religious community is free to observe its holidays and weekly day of rest and to administer its internal affairs. Each has its own religious council and courts, recognised by the law of Israel and with jurisdiction over all religious affairs.

There are nearly two million Arab citizens of Israel and there are more than 400 mosques in the state of Israel and are about 350 Muslim Imams who are getting their salaries and pension from the Israeli government. These Mosques are protected by the Jewish State and their Muslim citizens have full and equal rights in the state. They live side by side with their Jewish cousins in peace and unity.

Israel is home to a widely diverse population from many ethnic, religious, cultural and social backgrounds. The Israeli society is relatively young and is characterised by social and religious commitment, political ideology, economic resourcefulness and cultural creativity, all of which contribute momentum to its continuing development. Hundreds of Israeli Muslims serve in the IDF to protect their land of Israel and its people. While Muslims face many challenges across the globe one of them being Islam phobia we cannot stop and counter this hateful behaviour until we tackle the menace of anti-Semitism. Muslim and Jewish communities in the UK must unite and fight against the intolerance of anti-Semitism and Islam phobia. We need to sit together and listen to each other; we must never let the extremists win by spreading hate and creating division.

If ever there was a time to be a fundamentalist for peace, this is the time. If ever there was a need for fanatical belief in a shared future for Palestinians and Israelis, the need is now. There can be a peace process between Israelis and Palestinians but both nations need to work on it very seriously, there are barriers but it's not impossible at all. There are always two kinds of people in the world: Those who believe in the possibility of peace and those who do not.

An apology and Forgiveness will be central to progress, without forgiveness, no any peace plan will work. The apology was a key to peace in South Africa and both nations, Israelis and Palestinians should forgive each other and take a positive step in future. Recognition and Acceptances are just as important. Palestinians and Arabs have to accept Israel as a Jewish state. The Palestinians must recognize the Jewish historical, religious and emotional connection to the Temple Mount. This is consistent with Islamic traditions. At the same time, Israelis have to accept that there is a Palestinian people—not merely "West Bankers"— and acknowledge the historical memory of the Palestinians even it is only a 70-year-old but the reality is this they exist now. Israel must also see it as a Middle Eastern country, not a western country. Through mutual religious tolerance, great progress can be made, though the anti-peace groups will do everything to brainwash, blackmail and persuade us that peace is not possible. I hope, we can educate a new generation in the language of peace and dialogue, rejecting the boycotts, barriers and divisions of the past.

Islam Supports Israel's Right of Existence[2]

It is mandatory upon all Muslims to support Israel and her right to exist in the holy land because the holy book of Islam, the Quran supports Israel. There are many verses in the Quran which support the divine right of Jews on the land of Israel but I want to quote only three to justify the right of the existence of Israel. The first verse of the Holy Quran stipulates:

"And we said thereafter to the Children of *Israel*, 'Dwell securely in the Promised Land" [3]

And the second orders the people of Bane-*Israel* to enter the Holy-Land:

"O my people (the Jews)! Enter the Holy Land, which God has assigned unto you"[4]

In the third verse, Allah Almighty orders the children of *Israel* to scatter and says:

"And we said to the Children of *Israel* afterwards, 'scatter and live all over the world... and when the end of the world is near, we will gather you again into the Promised Land" [5]

The above-cited Quranic verses are a solid proof that this land was divinely given to the people of Israel and Muslims have no religious or historical claim to possess this land. There are many religious Islamic scholars and secular Muslim modernists who not only showed their full support to Israel but proved through writing that Israelis have a historical and divine right to exist in the Promised Land. The land was promised to the Bane-Israel in the holy Torah and in the holy Quran respectively. There is little agreement among past or contemporary Islamic scholars and Muslim academics about the exact location of the "beautiful dwelling place" that Allah gave to the Jews. According to Muslim modernist writer Tarek Fatah:

---

2   Author's Public Speech in London

3   Quran: 17:104

4   Quran: 5:21

5   Quran: 17:104

"While al-Tabari's medieval commentary on this verse mentions Palestine and Jerusalem as the land of God assigned to the Jews, it also lists other possibilities, such as Mount Sinai "and that which is around it", Syria, Jericho, Damascus and Jorden." The land of Israel, which is mentioned as a Canaan in the Holy Quran referred to the Jews, the people of Israel and the descendants of Prophet Isaac (PBUH). However, the Arab land was given to the descendants of Prophet Ismail (PBUH), it's a bright truth which every Muslim should accept and support it. According to Pro. Sheikh Abdul Hadi Palazzi a lecturer in the Department of the History of Religion at the University of Velletri:

"God wanted to give Avraham a double blessing, through Ishmael and through Isaac, and ordered that Ishmael's descendants should live in the desert of Arabia and Isaac's in Canaan. The Quran recognizes the Land of Israel as the heritage of the Jews and it explains that, before the Last Judgment, Jews will return to dwell there. This prophecy has already been fulfilled."[6]There is an argument which still remains unanswered that which land, Allah promised to the people of Israel, a land which was the Kingdom of Israel (Eretz Yisrael) in back days or the land (State of Israel) which has new current borders? Sheikh Muhammad al-Husseini, a British imam who teaches a course on the Quran at the Leo Baeck College in London says:

"They are pointing to the same area; it is not Egypt, Saudi or Iraq". According to al-Husseini "The traditional commentators from the rights and the ninth century onwards have uniformly interpreted the Quran to say explicitly that Eretz Yisrael has been given by God to the Jewish people as a perpetual covenant. There is no Islamic counterclaim to the Land anywhere in the traditional corpus of commentary."I personally do not argue on the ancient borders of the kingdom of Israel but I must argue that every Muslim must accept the current borders of the state of Israel according to the teachings of Islam. The Quranic verse again and again reminds Muslims about the rightful owners. It says;"O' My people. Enter the Holy Land, which Allah has destined for you, and do not turn your back or you will turn about losers."

---

6   What the Qur'an really says by Sheikh Abdul Hadi Palazzi, Page 2

[7]One of the earliest commentaries on the Quran was made by the 18th century scholar Muqatil ibnSulayman. Sulayman said:Allah instructs Moses to order the Jews: "Do not retreat from that land, or you will be losers. This is because God said to Abraham, when he was in the Holy land, "Verily, this land is which you now stand will be an inheritance for your son after you.

Islam never claimed the land of Israel (Jerusalem) as its own but every time, it mentioned in the holy Quran that this land belongs to the Jews, the real owners of the land. It is a bitter truth that the Dom of the Rock was built on the ruins of the Temple Mount by a Muslim caliph Abdul-Malik in 691 CE. The Dome of the Rock is situated in the centre of the Temple Mount, the site of the Temple of Solomon and the Jewish Second Temple. Now, the question remained unanswered that does Muslim caliph Abdul-Malik had a right to build the Dom of the Rock on the central point of the Jewish holy temple? Absolutely no. Muslims have no any divine or historical right to build the Dom of the Rock on the ruins of the Temple Mount which was the holy Ka'abah for the Jewish people (Bane Israel). According to Khaleel Mohammad, Professor of Religion at San Diego State University:

"When I tell people that the medieval Muslims – based on the Quran – were happy to look forward to the resettlement of Israel by Jews, and that the Caliph Omar called the land a *Waqf* (trust) because he knew it was not territory to be conquered, but saw it as a land to be held in trust for its rightful owners, they look at me as if I am from outer space."[8]I have always mentioned in my previous articles published in various newspapers that the Palestine and Israel conflict were actually political, but it was dragged in the religious way, because the Muslims rulers and leaders knew, they cannot beat the state of Israel on the grounds of nationalism so they decided to bring so called religious Jihad against the state of Israel.

They were successfully achieved a political goal through waging

---

7   Quran: 5:21

8   http://www.ibtimes.co.uk/quran-supports-israel-so-why-are-so-many-muslims-anti-semitic-1557446

so called holy Jihad to create a chaos and fear within the Israeli community through Political Islamic Extremist movements such as Hamas, Hezbollah and many others. Professor Khaleel Mohammad further says on this conflict:"After the Arabs lost the Six-Day War, Islamic scholars convened in Cairo and tried to make Palestine into a Muslim cause, realising that Arab nationalism was not enough to forge a strong alliance. Among the resolutions of the conference was to basically create a state of jihad."[9]

Extreme religious clerics teach Muslims that Islam forbids friendships with Yahud (Jews) and Nasarah (Christians), which I believe is a pure political Islamic rhetoric nothing else. Most of the Islamic countries have strong relations and most of the Muslims in the world have good friendships with Christians.

They have a religious and political cohesion among each other and they do not even bather the warning given by the Extremist clerics that Islam forbids friendships with Christians, but whenever these relations turn into the direction of Israel and to the people of Israel, all Muslims recall what Allah ordered them not to make friendships with yahud (Jews). This is a pure political and religious hypocrisy in the Muslim world. The reality is far different. The Quran says:...Likewise, you are permitted to marry chaste believing women [Muslims] or chaste women among the people who were given the Scripture [Jews and Christians] ...[10]

This is how contradictory concepts of some scholars create misunderstanding between the Jews and Muslims by issuing statements that Allah forbids friendships with Jews. On one hand Allah says Muslims can marry with the Jewish women and on the other hand Allah says we cannot make friendship with Jews. How contradictory is that! The fact of the matter is that Allah never said this. There is no contradiction between both verses but we have a lack of knowledge to understand the real face of Islam and the true teaching of the Quran. In reality, the Quran never

---

9   Ibid

10 Quran: 5:05

ordered that we cannot make friendship with Jews. Let's read what the real position of Islam on this issue is: Extremist clerics mention the verse of the holy Quran:

"O' YOU who have obtained faith! Do not take the Jews and the Christians for your allies: they are but allies of one another and whoever of you allies himself with them becomes verily one of them; behold, God does not guide people who are unjust." [11]

This verse is often quoted to show that Islam is intolerant. A complete understanding can only be achieved by understanding the whole issue as presented over all the verses and chapters and not by looking at only part of the Quran. God specifically warns us against doing just that, upholding part of the Quran while disregarding the rest. During the time of the Prophet Muhammad (PBUH) when the Jews and Christians were in open conflict with the Muslims, there were some Muslims who were more concerned about maintaining their alliances with the Jews and Christians at the expense of the Muslim community. The above verse is referring to such situations where Muslims with doubts in their hearts will ally themselves with the enemy. Let us look at some other verse about this issue. The following verse regulates relations with some people, regardless of faith: As for such [of the unbelievers] as do not fight against you on account of [your] faith, and neither drive you forth from your homelands, God does not forbid you to show them kindness and to behave towards them with full equity: for verily, God loves those who act equitably. [12]

From the above verse, we learn that we are only discouraged from befriending those who fight Muslims because of their religion. So, according to the above verses from the Quran, you can be kind to Jews, you can have Jewish friends and you can have a good relationship with Jews except those who fight with you. Muslims have many similarities with the Jewish religion and we are not forbidden to make friendship or marry with the Jewish people. Allah has made our relations strong by instructing to marry

---

11 Quran: 5:51

12 Quran: 60:8

with the Jewish women. We are very closest allies religiously and politically in the world, especially in the Europe. We should not fight but to unite each other through religious and political gatherings.

According to Imam Abdullah Antepli, the architect of the programme Muslim Leadership Initiative:"Jewish and Muslim communities in Europe and North America are the closest natural allies to each other. They have so many common challenges and so many common opportunities to thrive together. So far, both communities seem to ignore each other or fight – figuratively speaking – the proxy war of the Israel-Palestine conflict."Moreover – and those who try to use Islam as a weapon against Israel always conveniently ignore this point – the Holy Qur'an explicitly refers to the return of the Jews to the Land of Israel before the Last Judgment – where it says: "And thereafter We [Allah] said to the Children of Israel: 'Dwell securely in the Promised Land. And when the last warning will come to pass, we will gather you together in a mingled crowd.'".[13] Therefore, from an Islamic point of view, there is NO fundamental reason which prohibits Muslims from recognizing Israel as a friendly State. In the end, I want to quote another verse from the Holy Quran, which clearly says:"O Children of Israel, remember my favour that I have bestowed upon you and that I preferred you over the worlds" [14]

---

13 Qur'an 17:104

14 Quran: 2:47

CHAPTER 7

INTERNATIONAL HATRED AGAINST
THE STATE OF ISRAEL

The UNSC Resolution, Pope Francis and the French Summit

Social, electronic and print media against Israel had been heating up regarding UNSC (UN Security Council) Resolution 2334 that was passed against the state of Israel.[1] I saw many people jumping and giggling around as they believed they defeated Israel as a result of the UNSC resolution. UNSC Resolution 2334 was passed in order to continue to give Israel a hard time on the international political stage and provide more room for those who wish to demonise Israel and single out Israelis around the world. I believe, there are some concerns about the settlement policies in Israel, but these policies must be dealt with through dialogue between the Palestinian Authority (PA) and Israel. These resolutions have absolutely no legal grounds to implement, but are considered as condemnation of Israel.

Hundreds of resolutions have been passed against the state of Israel in relation to the Palestinian issue and there are about 77 resolutions which condemned Israel directly between 1955 to 2013 but ONLY one UNSC resolution, 1435, was passed against the Palestinians, which was "... 'calls on' the Palestinian Authority to meet its expressed commitment to ensure that those responsible for terrorist acts are brought to justice by

---

1   https://www.theguardian.com/world/2016/dec/23/us-abstention-allows-un-to-demand-end-to-israeli-settlements

112

it".[2] This is a clearly demonstrates the plain hatred of Israel by the UN and it proved that these international game players support Palestinian terrorism against the democratic state of Israel. One resolution compared to hundreds against Israel justify that those countries who voted on the resolution 2334 do not want to maintain peace in the region and no doubt that these countries are involved in the Middle East's chaotic situation. It was an absurd and monstrous act committed by the UNSC.

The world must realise that in the last few decades, the UN passed only eight resolutions against Syria, the country that killed nearly one million of their own people and more than 200 resolutions passed against Israel,[3] the only country where people from every race, gender and religion feel safe and live in peace. This is a blatant hypocrisy and insane. It was not the first time that the US abstained rather than vetoed a resolution (it has done so 20 times before with the seven under Reagan being the highest) prior to UNSC resolution 2334 but there are resolutions that the US remained abstained and given a final push in passing them against the state of Israel in a different US presidential area. The US has also voted 24 times to condemn Bush Sr. heading the list with 9 of them. The UNSC resolution 2334 was a direct condemnation of (illegal according to the UN) Jewish settlements by the state of Israel. However, we wish to see the resolution passed against the illegal Palestinian settlements in and around the city of Jerusalem and in the "C" area of the Judea and Samaria, which is legally controlled by the state of Israel according to the Oslo Accords Agreement.

Those people who consider settlement as the prime barrier to the peace between Israel and the Palestinians are ignorant of the history and remain in the dark about the current situation in the region. Israel removed all Jewish settlements and its entire security force from the Gaza strip in 2005 and yet the country and the nation suffers from the heat of terrorism, and Hamas

---

2   https://2001-2009.state.gov/p/nea/rt/15671.htm

3   https://sethfrantzman.com/2016/12/24/abstaining-from-history-heres-all-the-un-resolutions-on-israel-the-us-abstained-on/

has continued to be vocal about its desire to destroy Israel and every Jew. The Jewish settlements are not the barrier, but an unresolved and disputed conflict is the main barrier to the peace in the light of the UN interfering. Where is the resolution against the Hamas to impede her from terrorism? Where is the resolution that prevents the rest of the world by providing financial aid that has turned into payment to terrorists for rewards who to those who killed Israeli civilians? Where is the resolution that forces the PA to organise one and again have peace talks with Israel?

Peace cannot be achieved until international bodies stop interfering in this complicated matter, let both parties sit together and find a peaceful solution. The Palestinian Authority President Mahmood Abbas threatened Israel with bloodshed if the US embassy was ever shifted from Tel Aviv to Jerusalem. Bloodshed is not a positive solution between two peoples, it is not a resolution of the ongoing conflict, and a peaceful negotiation is the ONLY one which comprises the interests of both peoples.

Very soon after passing resolution 2334 in the UNSC, European Union (EU) countries held an International Peace Summit in France,[4] supposedly to find a two-state solution of this conflict. I strongly condemn this one-sided conference, which was only to pressure Israel to accept the two-state solution with the non-parallel condition of the Palestinian Authority. The solution cannot be achieved that is one-sided, both parties need to sit down and find a long-lasting peace for both peoples. The EU countries are playing a biased character political game which will create more fear for the people of both sides and will endanger the Middle Eastern peace. The French Summit to me is no different than the conference (Wannsee Conference) which was held in Germany by the Nazis against the Jewish people.

The strange thing was the announcement of the Vatican City to establish the embassy of Palestine. This was completely ridiculous to me that the Pope Francis was going to establish the embassy for an area which has not a legal status only as a territory first of Rome, then the Ottoman Empire and finally the UK, since 135

---

4   The Times of Israel, 22 Dec 2016

CE. This was nothing but to provide new oxygen to anti-Israel and anti-Zionism elements. Tomorrow, if Hamas announced the establishment of the embassy of the Islamic State (IS) that covered the area equivalent to the United Kingdom (UK), would the international community approve it? It was Europe that exterminated 6,000,000 Jewish people in the World War II and many, many people still think of Pope Pius XII as a Hitler's Pope. It was the current Pope Francis, who said:

> "Dialogue is born from an attitude of respect for the other person, from a conviction that the other person has something good to say. It assumes that there is room in the heart for the person's point of view, opinion, and proposal. Dialogue entails a cordial reception, not a prior condemnation. In order to dialogue it is necessary to know how to lower the defences, open the doors of the house, and offer human warmth."[5]

But Pope proved himself wrong when he committed himself to one side and announced the opening an embassy of the state of Palestine (not a state yet) without consulting Israel, (the prime associate of peace between both nations). Dialogue always carried on between two parties, but supporting only one party is an incitement against the other party. To stand against the state of Israel, the Pope rejected the doctrine of the Holy Bible, which reaffirms the right of Israelis in the Holy Land. He damaged the relationship between Christians and Jews. The Pope has no religious or political right to single out Israel the Holy Land. Instead, he should have called both country's representatives to his office to start new peace negotiations. Pope Francis should not forget that Jesus Christ, whom he worships, was a Jewish Rabbi, follower of the holy Torah and born in the land called Israel, not Palestine, according to the New Testament.

He has breached his religious code and has no legal and religious authority to remain as a Catholic Pope. He should not have involved his religious status in the Middle East politics if he cannot help to bring about peace in the region. The UN resolution, the one-sided European summit and the political announcement of the Catholic Church one right after another and their only

5   United States conference of Catholic Bishops, (USCCB), 2013, page 1

mission was to single out Israel, generate heat and opened the door to further provocation against the Jewish people all around the world. Are they going to repeat again the horrible and blood-stained European history against this person of the Levant? But they are forgetting that the Jewish people are not alone anymore and are not as weak as they were during World War II, but is now one of the most powerful nations in the Middle East and they know how to and will defend their country and the people.

The world should not forget that almost every latest technology they use is creations of Israel, by the same Israelis whom they hate most. The International community does not seem to remember that many of the most advanced military technologies they use to defend themselves are the invention of the state of Israel whom they demonise on the international political platform. I never consider Israel as a perfect country-such a thing does not exist-and there are certainly many political policies which need to be corrected, but obviously, it is as a democratic country as the UK. We must accept Israel with her positive and negative policies as we do in the UK and the US. We should promote Israel's positive and creative image to the world as a bright reality.

I recall when I attended Al Quds Day in Pakistan and in London, waving Hamas flags and chanting death to Israel, "Free Free Palestine." I never knew then, that today I would stand with Israel and the Jewish people and now chant, "Am Israel Chai." This seems like a really sweet dream. At that time, I stood with lies, hate, racism and Anti-Semitism, yet now I stand with truth, bright proof, against racism and Anti-Semitism. People, especially in the Muslim community do not know what Al Quds Day is. It's a day started by Iran and Hezbollah to address their hatred and racism against the State of Israel and the Jewish community in the world alike. This day has nothing to do with Sunni and Arab countries as it is marked by Iran after creating a so-called Islamic regime.

The UK's Muslim community organising and celebrating Al Quds for the last two decades, as far as I know, have absolutely no clue of the ideology behind marching on this day. Al-Quds Day was inaugurated in 1979 by Iran's supreme leader Ayatollah Khomeini to protest the existence of the State of Israel. Since then, Muslims, especially South Asians, Sunni and Shia, have been marching together to show the anger and racism against the legitimate and legal State of Israel. This day is held on every last Sunday of the Month of Ramadan as organised by the Iranian regime.

Surprisingly, UK's non-Muslim organisations are also among the organisers of this march and many followers of human rights' organisations attend the protest. It is not because they support Muslims but it is because they hate the Jewish people and their only country Israel.

They forget that this day was introduced in the country in which they live in peace and freedom to express their full human rights, by those that also want their death and destruction. The presence of Hezbollah supporters is a sign of terrorism in the UK. Hezbollah is declared one of the terrorist organisations among ISIS, Al-Qaeda and Hamas in the UK. Still, people celebrate Hezbollah and Hamas days (Al-Quds) in the western countries without noticing that there is no difference from ISIS, Al Qaeda, Hezbollah and Hamas. The rule of defining terrorist organisations does not distinguish between them, so, why would we? Because, we are blind in hatred of the Jewish people and forget whom we support.

How would you feel if someone waved a flag of ISIS in a rally or in a march in the streets of London? Obviously, it would create chaos among the UK population and it would generate a panic situation in the UK media and it would alert the UK security service. However, waving Hamas or Hezbollah flags would not bother any of them because it is against the State of Israel and against the Jewish people across the world? Hezbollah and Hamas are terrorist organisations under the schedule 2 of the Terrorism Act 2000. [6] Under the terrorism act, it is a criminal offence if someone promotes or encourages terrorism (Including the unlawful glorification of terrorism). So, in this case, waving

6   https://www.gov.uk/government/publications/proscribed-terror-groups-or-organisations--2

the flags of declared terrorist organisations in the streets of London falls under the definition of unlawful glorification of terrorism and the individual(s) who commit the offence must be dealt with by the UK security departments under the Act of Terrorism 2000. Hamas was declared a terrorist organisation in 2001 and Hezbollah 2001 and 2008 under the Terrorism Act 2000.

But there is a loophole in the UK law system which creates law enforcement departments' confusion in regards to how to react if someone flies the flag of terrorist organisations in the UK. It's hard to prove his action in the court whether he is a supporter, sympathiser or an active member of the proscribed terrorist organisation. Here are mentioned two different definitions of flying terrorist flags.

1. According to the Public Order Act 1986, which is implemented in England and Wales, someone is guilty of causing "harassment, alarm or distress" if they "display any writing, sign or other visible representation which is threatening or abusive with the hearing or sight of a person likely to be caused harassment, alarm or distress thereby." [7]

2. According to the Terrorism Act 2000, "A person in a public place commits an offence if he (a) wears an item of clothing, or (b) wears, carries or displays an article, in a such way or in such circumstances as to arouse reasonable suspicion that he is a member of supporter of a proscribed organisation." [8]

The Hezbollah organisation has been prescribed since 2001. This offence if proven guilty of terrorism under the Terrorism Act 2000, carries a person's sentence of up to six months and a fine. In fact, the London Mayor has no authority over our power to stop the Al-Quds protest because it comes under the European convention of human rights 1952, Article 10, Freedom of Expression and Article 11, Freedom of Assembly.

---

7   Proscribed Terrorist Organisations, Home office, Page 2

8   Ibid

118

Article 10 of the European Convention on Human Rights provides the right to freedom of expression and information, subject to certain restrictions that are "in accordance with law" and "necessary in a democratic society". This right includes the freedom to hold opinions, and to receive and impart information and ideas.

Article 11 of the European Convention on Human Rights protects the right to freedom of assembly and association, including the right to form trade unions, subject to certain restrictions that are "in accordance with law" and "necessary in a democratic society".

According to these human rights laws, as in the UK, it is hard for any authority to impose a ban on such marches and it is beyond the Mayor of London's powers to go over and impose sanctions on the protest whether it is the current Mayor, Sadiq Khan or Boris Johnson or any future Jewish Mayor.

But it is a prime responsibility of the office of Mayor and the London Metropolitan Police to make sure flags of terrorist organisations cannot be flown in the streets of London because the impact of waving flags of terrorist organisations would be intense and it would definitely generate extremism and racism against certain communities and country.

Mayor Sadiq Kahn is working hard with the Jewish community, providing reassurance that any act of Anti-Semitism would not be welcomed by him and would be dealt according the law. Yet, waving Hamas and Hezbollah flags in his jurisdiction would send a negative message to the London Jewish community. This act will surely damage the positive efforts of Sadiq Khan and will break Jewish trust with him. Therefore, this is a prime opportunity for the Mayor of London, Sadiq Khan, to prove himself and that the matters of the Jewish community in England and their concerns are most important for him and would be taken seriously.

AL QUDS DAY: Waving Hezbollah Flags in London

I recall when I attended Al Quds Day in Pakistan and in London,

119

waving Hamas flags and chanting death to Israel, "Free Free Palestine." I never knew then, that today I would stand with Israel and the Jewish people and now chant, "Am Israel Chai." This seems like a really sweet dream. At that time, I stood with lies, hate, racism and Anti-Semitism, yet now I stand with truth, bright proof, against racism and Anti-Semitism. People especially in the Muslim community do not know what Al Quds Day is. It's a day started by Iran and Hezbollah to address their hatred and racism against the State of Israel and the Jewish community in the world alike. This day has nothing to do with Sunni and Arab countries as it is marked by Iran after creating a so-called Islamic regime.

The UK's Muslim community organising and celebrating Al Quds for the last two decades, as far as I know, have absolutely no clue of the ideology behind marching on this day. Al-Quds Day was inaugurated in 1979 by Iran's supreme leader Ayatollah Khomeini to protest the existence of the State of Israel. Since then, Muslims, especially South Asians, Sunni and Shia, have been marching together to show the anger and racism against the legitimate and legal State of Israel. This day is held on every last Sunday of the Month of Ramadan as organised by the Iranian regime.

Surprisingly, UK's non-Muslim organisations are also among the organisers of this march and many followers of human rights' organisations attend the protest.

It is not because they support Muslims but it is because they hate the Jewish people and their only country Israel. They forget that this day was introduced in the country in which they live in peace and freedom to express their full human rights, by those that also want their death and destruction.

The presence of Hezbollah supporters is a sign of terrorism in the UK. Hezbollah is declared one of the terrorist organisations among ISIS, Al-Qaeda and Hamas in the UK. Still, people celebrate Hezbollah and Hamas days (Al-Quds) in the western countries without noticing that there is no difference from ISIS, Al Qaeda, Hezbollah and Hamas. The rule of defining terrorist organisations does not distinguish between them, so, why would we? Because, we are blind in hatred of the Jewish people and forget whom we support. How would you feel if someone waved a flag of ISIS in a rally or in a march in the streets of London? Obviously, it would create chaos among the UK population and it would generate a panic situation in the UK media and it would alert the UK security service.

However, waving Hamas or Hezbollah flags would not bother any of them because it is against the State of Israel and against the Jewish people across the world? Hezbollah and Hamas are terrorist organisations under the schedule 2 of the Terrorism Act 2000. Under the terrorism act, it is a criminal offence if someone promotes or encourages terrorism (Including the unlawful glorification of terrorism). So, in this case, waving the flags of declared terrorist organisations in the streets of London falls under the definition of unlawful glorification of terrorism and the individual(s) who commit the offence must be dealt with by the UK security departments under the Act of Terrorism 2000. Hamas was declared a terrorist organisation in 2001 and Hezbollah 2001 and 2008 under the Terrorism Act 2000. [9]

But there is a loophole in the UK law system which creates law enforcement departments confusion in regards to how to react if someone flies the flag of terrorist organisations in the UK. It's hard to prove his action in the court whether he is a supporter, sympathiser or an active member of the prescribed terrorist organisation. Here mentioned are two different definitions of flying terrorist flags.

1. According to the **Public Order Act 1986**, which is implemented in England and Wales, someone is guilty of causing "harassment, alarm or distress" if they "display any writing, sign or other visible representation which is threatening or abusive with the hearing or sight of a person likely to be caused harassment, alarm or distress thereby." [10]

---

9   Proscribed Terrorist Organisations, Home office, Page 9-10

10   Proscribed Terrorist Organisations, Home office, Page 14-15

2. According to the **Terrorism Act 2000**, "A person in a public place commits an offence if he (a) wears an item of clothing, or (b) wears, carries or displays an article, in a such way or in such circumstances as to arouse reasonable suspicion that he is a member of supporter of a proscribed organisation."[11]

The Hezbollah organisation has been **prescribed since 2001**. This offence if proven guilty of terrorism under the Terrorism Act 2000, carries a person's sentence of up to six months and a fine.

In fact, the London Mayor has no authority over our power to stop the Al-Quds protest because it comes under the European convention of human rights 1952, Article 10, **Freedom of Expression** and Article 11, **Freedom of Assembly**.

Article 10 of the European Convention on Human Rights provides the right to freedom of expression and information, subject to certain restrictions that are "in accordance with law" and "necessary in a democratic society". This right includes the freedom to hold opinions, and to receive and impart information and ideas.

Article 11 of the European Convention on Human Rights protects the right to freedom of assembly and association, including the right to form trade unions, subject to certain restrictions that are "in accordance with law" and "necessary in a democratic society".

According to these human rights laws, as in the UK, it is hard for any authority to impose a ban on such marches and it is beyond the Mayor of London's powers to go over and impose sanctions on the protest whether it is the current Mayor, Sadiq Khan or Boris Johnson or any future Jewish Mayor. But it is a prime responsibility of the office of Mayor and the London Metropolitan Police to make sure flags of terrorist organisations cannot be flown in the streets of London because the impact of waving flags of terrorist organisations would be intense and it would definitely generate

---

11 Ibid

extremism and racism against certain communities and country.

Mayor Sadiq Kahn is working hard with the Jewish community, providing reassurance that any act of Anti-Semitism would not be welcomed by him and would be dealt according the law. Yet, waving Hamas and Hezbollah flags in his jurisdiction would send a negative message to the London Jewish community.

This act will surely damage the positive efforts of Sadiq Khan and will break Jewish trust with him. Therefore, this is a prime opportunity for the Mayor of London, Sadiq Khan, to prove himself and that the matters of the Jewish community in England and their concerns are most important for him and would be taken seriously.

'Kill the Jews' is a basic tool of terrorism

In every act of terrorism, there you find certain people reasoning and justifying it, and one of the main reasons behind every act of terrorism in the world is, JEWS. This is the reason, you will hear about and read from the Muslim community, whether they are in the West or in the East. I name their reason as Anti-Semitism, because without hating Jews, you cannot fulfil your political or religious extremism which easily leads you towards terrorism. Every Islamic terrorist possesses a hatred of Jews ideology, they openly glorify anti-Semitism, and it doesn't matter whether they are in religious places, in conferences, in the streets or in the field of terrorism (Jihad). You will certainly hear their famous slogan, Kill the Jews.

From my point of understanding, overwhelming Anti-Semitism is one of the prime and easiest tools of Islamic extremists and without possessing these filthy ideas, they cannot climb the next stage which is an act of violent extremism. Violent extremism can slowly turn into the act of terrorism and obviously, terrorist's first wish would be to harm Jews whenever and wherever they find them. Often living in close proximity, what easy targets they can make for terrorists to carry out their terror activity against the Jews community.

123

Now, the question is this, is Anti-Semitism a basic tool of terrorism? Of course; it is.

There are three stages for someone to become a potential religious terrorist.

1.   Hate.

2.   Extremism.

3.   Terrorism.

It depends on the person as to which type of hate he or she possesses inside and against whom, but I certainly assure you, that it does not matter the form of hate or extremism, the end of the target generally is to kill Jews. There are many examples. Terrorists one of the planned goals is to kill Jews, even though their larger mission is to target infidel governments and non-Muslims alike.

The ultimate wish is to target and kill as many Jews as possible Here I share some famous examples where Islamic terrorists deliberately targeted Jews which was not their direct mission but the part of their terror mission.

Mumbai Attack[12]

The world's infamous Pakistani based terrorist organisation LeT (Lashkar e Taiba) carried out a ruthless terrorist act against the Indian people in 2008 that every person is aware of. The direct mission was to kill as many Indians as they wanted because of traditional hatred felt by many Pakistani Muslims for the Hindu community in India. None-the-less, they purposely targeted Norman House, a famous Jewish religious and cultural place in India.

Surprisingly, rather than just immediately killing their victims, the terrorists brutally tortured the Jews (among of them two were Israelis) before executing them. Islamic Terrorists were more than happy to kill Jews than Indians in their mission, as it

---

12   *The Indian Express*, 3 November 2016

was revealed in a joint investigation by Israeli and Indian security services. If you study the Mumbai attack case, you would find their main target was theoretically was Indian people but they added another important mission in their bloody game and that was to kill Jews.

The French Attacks[13]

In 2012, a lone wolf Islamic terrorist, entered into the Jewish school in Toulouse, in southern France and killed four French Jews including three innocent children. This was a direct act of terrorism against the Jewish community. He just wanted to kill Jews because he thought it gave him an easy entry into Paradise by killing Jews. In 2015, the world was shocked when they turned on their TV sets and saw the horrifying news about the terrorist attack in the heart of a Paris suburb. An Islamic terrorist killed many innocent French citizens. The incident dramatically changed when they saw a terrorist enter into the Jewish supermarket, take hostages, many Jews and finally killed 4 of them, including Yoav Hattab, the son of the Chief Rabbi of Tunis Benjamin Hattab. This incident shocked the entire Jews community in the world, especially in the state of Israel. The main target of this attack was to make a statement to the French government and the French people, but again, this terrorist intentionally targeted the Jewish people in their ruthless attack. Committing this part of the terrorist act, he was generating more satisfaction for himself by targeting Jews. This was the all-encompassing hate he possessed inside his fanatical beliefs, only G-D knows for how long.

In 2016, a Muslim man with suspected terrorist ties stabbed three soldiers outside the Jewish community centre in Nice, France. In the city of Nice, there are around 220,000 Muslims and 80,000 Jews living within diverse communities. But, unfortunately the Jewish community that has lived there for hundreds of years now sees approximately 25-35 physical anti-Semitic attacks annually, according to SPCJ (French Jewish Security Service).

---

13   The New York Times, 20 March, 2012

2003 UK Affiliated Attack in Tel Aviv[14]

The names of Omar and Asif are two names that Israeli community would never forget. These British-born Muslims detonated themselves in Mike's Place in Tel Aviv a dance club in Israel and killed 3 and injured 55 innocent lives. The toll would have been higher but Omar Sharif's belt failed to explode. These two anti-Semitic boys intentionally committed a huge act of suicide terrorism in Israel. They travelled from Britain to Israel to harm Israeli civilians, civilians that had no way harmed them in Britain or elsewhere in the world. These British fanatics had crossed the border via Jordan, then spent some time in Gaza (Gaza was under Israeli administration at that time) where they prepared themselves to commit this act of terrorism against Israeli civilians.

In fact, these terrorists were radicalised in the UK by their family members, the Muslim community and by the excess of Islamic freedom in the country. Both Islamic terrorists were hardcore religious persons affiliated with the ultra-conservative Deobandi sect of Islam, which is widely practiced in south Asian countries of Pakistan and Afghanistan and in communities in the UK. Omar Sharif's wife, sister and brothers were changed in court as accessories for not disclosing his intention to commit suicide terrorism in Israel. Their family members were aware of his violent intentions against Israeli citizens and they chose to hide it until the mission had been accomplished.

These were obviously not only two British Muslims who were radicalised against the Jews/Israeli community but will I bet, 99% British Muslims hate Israel and celebrate every harm happens in Israel. These Muslims have been radicalised since they were still very young children. A prime example, we just saw in a Palestinians Expo 2017. Very young school-aged Muslim children wore camouflage dresses or T-Shirts covered with slogans including "Free Palestine" and "Free Gaza". The children were shouting along with their parents against the Jewish people

---

14   The Telegraph, 20 May 2003

outside the Expo event.[15]

Among these children, could one or more be another potentially violent extremist who will hope to inflict grievous harm to the Jewish community in the future? Nobody knows. But the way their parents teach them to have an intense hatred against the Jewish people from childhood on may lead any of them to become an Islamic terrorist whose one of the prime goals could have been 'Kill the Jews'.

This is why, I strongly believe that Anti-Semitism is a basic root that leads someone to commit an act of terrorism against the Jewish/Israeli community anywhere in the world. One way to avoid encouraging such type of violent attitude is, I believe, for the British government to ban events held in the streets of England in solidarity with Palestinians. These events cause an increase in the already too flourishing anti-Semitic atmosphere amongst British Muslims. The fact that every individual has to accept it that Anti-Semitism is a form of Terrorism.

---

15 http://www.theturbantimes.com/2017/07/14/in-london-15000-people-at-tend-largest-palestine-event-in-europe/

CHAPTER **8**

ISRAEL AND THE PALESTINIANS: A GUIDE TO THE DEBATE

Professor Alan Johnson

HISTORY

WHAT IS ZIONISM:

Zionism is the name given to the national liberation movement of the Jewish people, calling for the restoration of sovereign Jewish life in the land of Israel after 2000 years of exile and persecution. While many Jews had been expelled from Judea by the Romans in the first and second centuries, a continuous Jewish presence existed in the Holy Land throughout the ages, focused around the holy cities of Jerusalem, Tiberias, Safed and Hebron. The land of Israel – 'Zion' – has always been integral to Jewish religious, cultural and national life and has suffused the prayers and practices of Jews around the world.

Modern Zionism was a response to anti-semitism – Jew-hatred. The persecution of Jews was a constant of European life in the medieval period. In the modern period, anti-semitism took on new forms, such as the belief that Jews were racially inferior, or involved in a global conspiracy. Jews in Europe were subject to waves of pogroms and persecution in the late 19th and early 20th centuries, culminating in the Holocaust when six million Jews were murdered by the Nazis.

The establishment of the State of Israel in 1948 marked the realisation of Zionism's central political goal of attaining an internationally recognised, legally secured home for the Jewish people, where Jews would be free from persecution and able to develop their national identity.

To describe Zionism as 'racist' is quite wrong. The charge is itself discriminatory because it denies to the Jewish people – and only the Jewish people – the right to national self-determination. Nationhood is a matter of self-definition, not external accreditation: the Jews see themselves as a people, with national rights, so whether others see them as only a religion is irrelevant. (Equally, anyone who says the Palestinians are not a people are quite wrong.)

Many of the Jews who moved to Palestine prior to the establishment of the State of Israel came as refugees fleeing persecution in various parts of Europe. They did not seek to subjugate the local population, but hoped that the lives of all the residents of the area would be improved by the influx of Jewish immigrants. Jews did not enter Palestine by force, but legally purchased land and built many new communities.

Mainstream Zionists always believed that a non-Jewish minority would live alongside the Jewish people as citizens with full and equal rights. This principle was enshrined in Israel's Declaration of Independence in 1948, which promised Arab inhabitants of the State of Israel 'full and equal citizenship and due representation in   all its provisional and permanent institutions.[1]

Was Israel established according to international law?

Yes. The right of the Jewish people to create a national home in Palestine was first recognised by the British in the 1917 Balfour Declaration, and then approved by the League of Nations (the forerunner of the United Nations) in 1922, with a ringing endorsement of 'the historical connection of the Jewish people with Palestine' and on the grounds for 'reconstituting their

---

1   BICOM, Israel: Frequently Asked Questions, London,2016.

national home in that country'.

In 1947, the General Assembly of the United Nations passed Resolution 181 which approved the partition of Mandate Palestine into 'Independent Arab and Jewish States.' The Jewish leadership in Palestine accepted the UN plan, even though the borders for the Jewish state were drawn with no consideration for its security, were virtually indefensible, and included a lot of desert. The UN partition resolution used the expression 'Jewish state' no fewer than 27 times.

The Partition Plan also gave the Arab community of Palestine a state and the opportunity for self-determination. Tragically, Palestinian leaders and the wider Arab world decided to reject the UN proposal and instead wage (and lose) a war against the infant Jewish state created by the UN. In 1949 a two-thirds majority at the United Nations accepted Israel as a full member. If the Arab world had also accepted the UN partition plan in 1947, Palestine would now be 69 years old.[2]

I have been told that the Jews 'ethnically cleansed' the Palestinians in 1948. What happened?

A civil war immediately followed the Palestinian Arab rejection of the Partition Plan, with Palestinian Arabs forming a guerrilla army and launching attacks on Jewish communities. Atrocities took place on both sides. The atrocity committed by Jewish forces at Deir Yassin was followed a few days later by the massacre of 78 Jewish academics, doctors and nurses travelling to Mt. Scopus carried out by Arabs. A few weeks after that, a day before Israel declared independence, 127 Jewish men and women were massacred in KfarEtzion after surrendering and laying down their arms.[3]

After the British left in 1948, and the Jewish community declared the establishment of Israel in line with the UN partition resolution, five Arab armies immediately invaded, intending to crush the

---

2 BICOM, Israel: Frequently Asked Questions, London, 2016.

3 Yair Sheleg, 'The death and rebirth of Kfar Etzion'. Haaretz, 3 May 2007.

Jewish state at birth and 'drive the Jews into the sea.' The Jews of Palestine were forced to fight back. They waged a defensive war for their survival, a mere three years after the Holocaust.

Between November 1947 and the end of the war in March 1949 approximately 750,000 Palestinian Arabs fled their homes and became refugees. With war raging, the factors that caused them to flee were complex. The historian Benny Morris, in his detailed and highly praised book 1948, concludes that 'The Palestinian refugee problem was born of war, not by design, Jewish or Arab' (emphasis added). That's the crux of the matter. Morris goes on: 'It was largely a by-product of Arab and Jewish fears and of the protracted, bitter fighting that characterised the first Israeli-Arab war.'[4] In the midst of the conflict, Israel's Declaration of Independence offered full citizenship and equal rights to all Arabs living within Israel. After the war, the 150,000 Arabs that remained in Israel were granted full citizenship. Arab members were elected to Israel's first parliament in 1949.

A future peace deal will have to define a just and viable solution for the Palestinian refugees while preserving the democratic principle of 'two-states for two peoples.

PEACE

Does Israel seek peace with the Palestinians?

Yes. Israel seeks peace, but peace with security. Israel wants peaceful relations with the Palestinians and all its neighbours, but it won't commit national suicide. All Israel asks is that its neighbours acknowledge the right of Israel's citizens to live in peace. No more rockets, no more terror tunnels, no more suicide bombers.

How has Israel sought peace with the Palestinians?

Israel has sought peace with the Palestinians through the

---

4 Benny Morris, The Birth of the Palestinian Refugee Problem, 1947-1949. Cambridge, 1989, 286.

negotiated two-state solution–the agreed division of the small strip of land between the River Jordan and the Mediterranean Sea into a Palestinian state alongside Israel. But Israel will not accept the creation of a Palestinian state instead of Israel or at war with Israel.

Three times in recent times Israel offered the Palestinians an independent state, in the West Bank and Gaza, with east Jerusalem as its capital and billions of dollars in international aid.

Three times the Palestinian government said no or failed to respond at all. Israel is eager to negotiate. Israel will sign a peace agreement that will turn over disputed land as soon as the Palestinian leaders recognise Israel as a Jewish state and accept its right to exist in peace.

Everyone has so much to gain from peace.

Why is the two-state solution the best way to secure peace between Israelis and Palestinians?

Because only the two-state solution is a solution to three things.[5]

First, the two-state solution solves the Palestinians' need for a state of their own in which to exercise their right to national self-determination as a people: it creates Palestine.

Second, the two-state solution solves the need of the Jewish people for a homeland, a place in which to express their right to national self-determination as a people: it secures Israel.

Third, the two-state solution, and only that solution, faces up to fact that both peoples seek to exercise their right to national self-determination in the same narrow strip of land.

Unless one people drives the other out and takes all the land for itself – unachievable without human suffering on a massive scale, but the dream of extremists on both sides, sadly–the only alternative is to negotiate a division of that land.

---

5   Fathom eBook, Two States for Two Peoples – 20 Years after Oslo II: How to renew the peace process between Israel and the Palestinians, 2015.

On campus, the Israel-Palestine debate is often treated as a Hollywood movie, with goodies and baddies. The real world is more complicated. Two legitimate claims to the same land must be reconciled through deep mutual recognition, painful compromise, mutual security guarantees, the division of the land into two-states, and peaceful coexistence.[6]

20 years of negotiations have not led to the two-state solution. Is it still viable?

Yes, for 6 reasons.

First, despite everything, Israelis and Palestinians still support the two-state solution, as the polls confirm.

Second, the international community – with its diplomatic weight, its capacity to legitimise a deal and its material resources to support the fledgling Palestinian state – still supports the two-state solution.

Third, the Arab League – a diplomatic grouping of the Arab states – supports the two-state solution. The 2002 Arab Peace Initiative – which offers recognition to Israel in return for a two-state deal along the 1967 lines – was renewed in 2013 with an amendment; the principle of 'land swaps' between Israel and Palestine was accepted. This matters hugely for two reasons: the Palestinians need the regional diplomatic   cover to make the two-state deal; the Israelis need the regional buy-in to take the tremendous security risks involved in making the two-state deal.

Fourth, both leaders, Mahmoud Abbas and Benjamin Netanyahu, are still (reluctant) two-staters. Abbas gave a television interview in 2012 to Israel's Channel 2 which he said, 'Look, I want to visit the village I was born in, Safed, but I know I can't go back to live there.' He has declared that for him Palestine is the West Bank and Gaza 'now and forever'. Benjamin Netanyahu committed himself to the two-state solution in a speech at Bar Ilan University in 2009. He reaffirmed that commitment during President Obama's

---

6   Alan Johnson, 'The Two State Solution is the only solution' (Cambridge Union debate), We Believe in Israel, 2013.

visit to Israel in 2013, saying he is ready to make a 'historic compromise' in order to 'end the conflict'. Although he does not think the security situation is conducive to a two-state solution tomorrow, he has said he remains committed to it because he has no intention of allowing Israel to drift into bi- nationalism.

Fifth, the gaps between the two parties have narrowed dramatically in the last 20 years. We have gone from a situation where it is a criminal offence for an Israeli to speak to the Palestinian Liberation Organisation to a handshake on the White House lawn between an Israeli prime minister and the PLO chairman. We have gone from the two-state solution being a fringe idea to it being the only serious policy framework, accepted as the way forward across enough of the political spectrum for it to happen– in Israel, Palestine, the Arab world, the US, and Europe.[7]

Sixth, settlements have not killed the two-state solution. The expert Shaul Arieli points out that 80 per cent of the settlers live in large 'blocs' close to the Green Line.

To connect those blocs up to what Michael Walzer calls 'Little Israel' will require a land swap of about 6 per cent. That is possible and the principle of land swaps is supported by Obama, the EU and the now Arab League. 20 per cent of the settlers live outside these green line blocs, often dotted around Route 60, the ridge running down the West Bank from North to South. These settlements will not be part of Israel after a deal. Between 20-30,000 households will have to be absorbed back into Israel (not the half a million people of legend).[8]

Is that scale of absorption of settlers doable?

Yes. Israel does absorption. Israel's population doubled from 4 to 8 million since 1980. Israel also does disengagement: from Sinai, Southern Lebanon, Gaza, and the northern West Bank. And the

---

7   Alan Johnson, 'The case for scrupulous optimism in the Middle East', Prospect, 4 July 2013.

8   ShaulArieli, why settlements have not killed the two-state solution, BICOM Expert View, 2013.

Israeli Defence Forces–religious soldiers included–does forcible disengagement. Settlers who had lived in Gaza for decades were removed within one week. Traumatic, for sure, but it happened once the political leadership declared it policy and the majority of Israelis believed it was in the national interest.

Yes, the challenges ahead remain huge. No, settlements have not killed the two- state solution – they have not even come close.

But is Israel really serious about peace?

Yes. Israel has repeatedly tried to make peace with its Arab neighbours based on the principle of 'land for peace.' Let's review the record.

The Zionist movement in Palestine accepted the 'two-states for two peoples' solution when it was first proposed by the British Peel Commission in 1937. Tragically, the Arabs rejected that solution.

The Zionist movement in Palestine accepted the United Nations Partition Plan in 1947, which would have created an Israel and a Palestine. Tragically, the Arabs rejected the UN Plan.

In 1967, in the immediate aftermath of the defensive Six-Day War – sparked by Arab armies once again massing on the borders of the Jewish homeland and issuing blood- curdling threats to 'drive the Jews into the sea' – Israel hoped that the Arab states would seek peace in return for Israeli withdrawal from the territory it had captured.

Again, the opportunity was missed. In September 1967, at a conference in Khartoum, the Arab League made its famous 'three NO's' declaration: No Peace with Israel, No Recognition of Israel and No Negotiation with Israel.

Israel returned the Sinai Peninsula to Egypt in return for peace and recognition in 1979. Egyptian President Anwar Sadat came to Israel and was cheered when he said 'No more war, no more bloodshed'.

Israel withdrew from Palestinian population centers in Gaza and the West Bank as part of the Oslo Accords with the PLO, signed in 1993.

Israel made territorial concessions to Jordan as part of the 1994 peace treaty between the two countries.

At the Camp David peace talks in 2000, the Israeli Prime Minister Ehud Barack tried to negotiate the creation of a Palestinian state. US President Bill Clinton supported this effort and took part in the talks. Clinton proposed two-states: a Palestinian state in 94 per cent of the West Bank plus an additional swap of land, and a sovereign capital in East Jerusalem. Israel broadly accepted this proposal but it was rejected by Palestinian leader Yasser Arafat, who made no counter-offer.[9]

In 2000, Israel complied with United Nations Security Council resolutions relating to Lebanon by withdrawing all its forces from south Lebanon.

In 2005, Israel withdrew unilaterally from the Gaza Strip and part of the northern West Bank, uprooting 8000 Jewish settlers, many forcibly.

- A Palestinian state in 93.7 percent of the West Bank and the whole of Gaza

- A compensating land swap: Israeli land–equivalent to 5.8 percent of the West Bank–transferred to the new Palestinian state.

- A land corridor across Israel connecting the West Bank and Gaza Strip.

- The Palestinian capital in East Jerusalem, as the Palestinians wanted.

- An international consortium of countries, including Jordan and Saudi Arabia, to work with both parties to

9   See DennisRoss, The Missing Peace: The Inside Story of the Fight for Middle East Peace, NewYork, Farrar Strauss, 2005; Joseph Federman, 'Abbas admits he rejected 2008 peace offer from Olmert', Times of Israel, 9 November2015.

address future arrangements for the Old City and its holy sites.

In 2008 Israel made it's most comprehensive peace offer yet to the Palestinians at the Annapolis Peace Talks. Ehud Olmert, the Israeli Prime Minister, proposed:

This was a serious, comprehensive offer from the Israeli side to make peace, and for many Israelis something of a litmus test as to whether it had a partner for peace.

Mahmoud Abbas, now President of the Palestinian Authority, did not respond to Israel's offer.

And once again, a Palestinian leader made no counter offer.

In 2013 the US Secretary of State John Kerry tried once more, inviting both parties to peace talks. After months of negotiations, Israel indicated its assent to a 'framework agreement'–a set of broad parameters for resolving the conflict – that John Kerry set down as a basis for continuing the talks. US President Obama met with the Palestinian President Mahmoud Abbas in the Oval Office and pleaded with him to do likewise.

Abbas, yet again, walked away, never getting back to Obama. He signed a unity agreement with Hamas instead.

Today, the Israeli Prime Minister continues to call for the talks to restart without preconditions, 'tomorrow, in Ramallah'. 'I don't want to govern the Palestinians,' he   says. 'I don't want them as subjects of Israel or as citizens of Israel. I want them to have their own independent state ... But there are necessary compromises on the Palestinian side ... peace is always a two-way compromise.[10]

Every Israeli government since 2000 has endorsed the two-state solution. The Israeli people back the two-state solution by a two-thirds majority.

Many people – including many people in Israel – feel that Israel

---

10   Barak Ravid, 'Netanyahu Says Willing to Meet with Abbas Any Time, but Without Preconditions', Haaretz, 06 September 2016.

could do even more to promote peace. Many want to see a settlement freeze now. But laying the responsibility for the failure, thus far, to reach a peace agreement solely at Israel's feet ignores the historical record.

Why are negotiations even needed? Why doesn't Israel simply get out of the West Bank and so end the occupation?

Because it would be too risky to walkout of the West Bank without negotiated security guarantees.

For many people all that matter is the occupation. That is understandable. The Palestinians have neither a vote nor a state of their own, nor the dignity that comes with having both. And in 2017 we will mark the 50th anniversary of the occupation.

The Palestinian people have a right to that state. The current situation is not sustainable, and the danger of a drift into a third intifada is ever-present. The stabbing intifada is the product not just of incitement – though the level of official and unofficial anti-semitic incitement is disgraceful – but also of hopelessness and frustration at occupation, statelessness and humiliation.

However, for Israel to 'just get out' of the West Bank without any security guarantees or a negotiated final status agreement would be to risk the very existence of the state of Israel. That is because the West Bank is the strategically critical high ground overlooking Israel's narrow coastal plain where most of its population and industry, and its only major international airport, are situated. A risky unilateral withdrawal from the high ground of the West Bank could be followed by a Hamas, or Jihadi takeover of the West Bank and its conversion into an Iranian-supplied rocket base from which missiles could rain down on Israeli cities.

These Israeli fears are not an 'excuse' as the campus extremists say. That is an example of 'decontextualising to demonise'. The Israeli fears are reasonable. Again, there is a record.

Israel 'just got out' of a security zone it controlled in Southern Lebanon in 2000 and there are now over 100,000 rockets aimed at

— 138

Israel in the hands of the anti-Semitic and terrorist organization Hezbollah, an Iranian proxy.

Israel 'just got out' of the Gaza Strip in 2005. Thousands of rockets have since been fired from the Strip on to Israeli civilians. And those rockets are getting more powerful. In November 2012 Iranian-supplied Farj-5 rockets with 70 km range fell on Tel Aviv and Jerusalem. As you read this, terror tunnels are being dug underneath Israel by Hamas to prepare a mass casualty terrorist attack.

And the security threat is not just from Hamas. Israelis see the entire Middle East disintegrating before their eyes. 'Iraq' does not really exist today. Nor does 'Syria' or 'Libya'. Israelis know that a few hours' drive away there is radical Islamism and Jihadism, the slaughter of minorities, waves of desperate refugees, and even child sex slave markets. This is the collapsing Middle East in which Israelis are being asked to   take a huge risk for peace and 'just get out' of the West Bank, hoping that its enemies will not just move in and continue the war against them.[11]

And of course, there is the radical Islamist and terror-sponsoring regime in Iran, whose foremost leaders continue to threaten to 'wipe Israel off the map'.[12]

So, as awful as it is that the occupation continues, Israelis have decided to seek to end the occupation by negotiations leading to a final status agreement over seen by the international community, not by a risky unilateral withdrawal from the West Bank without security guarantees or genuine mutual recognition.

Why can't Israel and Palestine just agree a 'One-State Solution'?

Some ideas, wrote George Orwell, are so absurd that you can only get the intellectuals to believe in them. The One State Solution is

---

11 Calev Ben-Dor, 'Can Israel remain secure in a world of Arab disintegration, American retreat, and Iranian ambition?', Fathom, Spring 2016.

12 Alan Johnson, Oral evidence to the Foreign Affairs Select Committee on UK policy towards Iran, 11 February 2014, Hansard.

one of those ideas.

The idea of creating a single state between the Jordan River and the Mediterranean Sea, in which Israelis and Palestinians will both give up sovereignty and merge the Israeli Defence Forces and the Al Aqsa Martyrs Brigade into one united and harmonious military force – is indeed absurd.

'One state' is anti-democratic and patronising:

The two peoples don't want the one-state solution. In 2012, a Gallup poll found that two thirds of Israelis and Palestinians want the two-state solution. One-staters in the Western universities simply ignore this. Left-wing Israeli writer Gadi Taubhas complained about this attitude: 'The natives – we Jews and Arabs – aspire to national self-determination. But the good 'old Brits, never tired of carrying the White Man's Burden, know that the natives are too barbaric to understand what the right form of self-determination should be for them.'

'One state' is politically impossible:

Given the century-long history of murderous conflict, forcing the two peoples into one state would be a recipe for permanent civil war. The one state solution ignores a century of bloody conflict in a well-meaning but willfully naïve John Lennon-esque spirit, singing 'imagine there's no countries, it's easy if you try'. This can't work because, as the Guardian journalist Jonathan Freedland puts it – and he is a sharp critic of Israeli governments, past and present – the one state solution is rather like advising a couple that can no longer bear the sight of each other that the answer is for them to get married.

The one state solution also flies in the face of recent history. The nation-state, far from being an 'anachronism' as the late historian Tony Judt once claimed, is going through a purple patch. Nation-states proliferated as the Soviet Union splintered, as Yugoslavia broke up, and in Eastern Europe when the wall fell. Even Czechoslovakia went for a peaceful two-state solution – dividing amicably into the Czech Republic and Slovakia–despite not having a century of murderous conflict behind them.

Cosmopolitan Europeans may think they have moved beyond the nation-state, but they should not demand everyone else does. And they really must stop demanding that the 69-year-old Jewish nation-state, set up after the Holocaust, should go first.

In the real world, the 'One state Solution' means violent conquest:

The core leaders of the BDS movement know that outside of seminar room discussions, the 'one state solution' means the conquest of Israel. That's for a simple reason: in the real world, and for obvious reasons, Israelis will never again put their fate in the hands of others. As for putting their fate in the hands of the Arab world, in the year 2016, well, the idea is ludicrous.

Some anti-Israel academics even admit that the one state solution can only be realised by violent conquest. Saree Makdisi, an English professor at UCLA, and a BDS leader, said, 'No privileged group in the history of the world has ever voluntarily renounced its privileges... the Israelis will never relinquish their privileges until they are compelled, preferable by non-violent means ... to accept the parameters of a single democratic state.' (That 'preferably' is a tissue-thin barrier to pogrom and conquest.)

The one-state solution also gets wrong what the conflict is actually about:

Two highly developed and distinct societies, Israeli and Palestinian, each based on a powerful sense of national identity, must divide the land. When there are strong desires for national self-determination the one-state idea collapses, the world over.

To divide the land each people needs to feel confident and secure if it is to make the necessary excruciating compromises. Each people must feel itself to be understood as a permanent feature of the Middle East. One-statism goes in the opposite direction. It proposes to resolve a national question by simply denying the right to national self-determination of both peoples!

GAZA

Why does Israel not just negotiate peace deal with Hamas, so there are no more conflicts? After all, you must negotiate peace with your enemies not with your friends.

Diplomacy is preferable to destruction. And all Israelis hope Hamas will reform. And Israel maintains a back channel to Hamas through Egypt to discuss cease fires when conflict breaks out. But right now, a full peace deal is out of reach because Hamas is a radical Islamist terror organization that thinks the destruction of Israelis a sacred duty.[13]

What you say about negotiations is true in most circumstances. But how do you negotiate with people who are committed, in principle, to your destruction – and teach that hatred to their children every day?

Hamas leaders repeatedly reject all possibility of a negotiated peace. They say in their founding Charter: 'There is no solution for the Palestinian question except through Jihad. Initiatives, proposals and international conferences are all a waste of time and vain endeavours.'

Israel wants to negotiate peace, but the Hamas Charter says: 'There is a Jew behind me, come on and kill him', 'There is no solution except by jihad' and 'so-called peaceful solutions are all contrary to the beliefs of [Hamas]'.

Hamas wants no state of Israel. Their Charter declares – on page one, line one – that 'Islam will obliterate Israel.' The Hamas Charter directs its followers to kill all Jews, whom are to blame for all the wars and revolutions, past and present. It is anti-semitic document. And it has never been renounced, despite what the campus apologists for Hamas claim.[14]

---

13 Matthew Levitt, Hamas: Politics, Charity and Terrorism in the service of Jihad, Yale, 2007; see also 'The state of Hamas: Toby Greene interviews BenedettaBerti',Fathom, Spring 2014.

14 The Hamas Covenant, The Covenant of the Islamic Resistance Movement, 18 August 1988, at Yale Law School Avalon Project.

What the Palestinians of Gaza and the West Bank should have is the opportunity for a two-state solution – a negotiated peace where Palestinians and Israelis agree to live next to each other in two separate states side by side in peace and security. If Hamas recognized Israel's right to exist, negotiations could be opened. But Hamas's then foreign minister Mahmoud al-Zahar has said: 'Israel is a vile entity that has been planted on our soil, and has no historical, religious or cultural legitimacy. We cannot normalise our relations with this entity... [We say] no to recognising Israel, regardless of the price we have to pay [for our refusal].'

We should not blame the people of Gaza for feelings of grief, anger and desperation. We should blame the Hamas leadership who sow the seeds of hate and tell innocent civilians to live as human shields while hiding in tunnels paid for by the international community. Why not build schools rather than tunnels?

We tend to treat pathological movements with no negotiable grievance as if they are rational political movements with grievances that can be negotiated. But not every terrorist group is the IRA in the 1990's, seeking to lay down its arms and negotiate a Good Friday Peace Agreement.

Paul Berman, author of Terror and Liberalism, warns about the 'rationalist naiveté' of many progressives in the West – we imagine that, deep down, everyone thinks just like us. But not everyone does, and our failure of imagination can make it impossible for us to grasp the nature of many modern extremist religious-political movements, especially radical Islamist movements like Hamas.

As Berman says, our rationalist naiveté stops us seeing that sometimes people 'behave in irrational ways or have succumbed to the allure of a cult of death'. When the Israelis turned over Gaza to the Palestinians, they turned over nearly 3,000 greenhouses and a thriving flower industry that would have earned Palestinians tens of millions of dollars in exports. What was the Palestinian government's response? The destruction of the 3,000 green houses and the impoverishment of its people.[15]

But aren't the Hamas rockets a defensive reaction to the Israeli blockade of the Gaza Strip?

No, they are not. It's actually the other way around. The Israeli (and Egyptian) imposed restrictions on what can enter the Gaza Strip as a defensive response to the Hamas rockets being fired on Israeli civilians.

Egypt has the exact same policy towards Hamas as Israel does: to stop the illegal tunnels and the illegal weapons.

The mistaken belief that the Israeli blockade came first misrepresents that blockade as, at best, a motiveless and cruel Israeli action, and at worst as positively demonic.

And it misrepresents the firing of Hamas rockets on Israeli civilians as heroic and understandable acts of resistance to a cruel and motiveless blockade.

The fallacy also leads people to think that if only Israel 'lifted the blockade' then peace would breakout.

This fallacy about the rockets being a response to the blockade rather than vice versa spreads because of what people don't know.

People do not know that when Israel left Gaza in 2005, the Israeli Prime Minister Ariel Sharon said: 'We desire a life living side-by-side, in understanding and peace. Our goal [in disengaging] is that the Palestinians will be able to live in dignity and freedom in an independent state, and, together with us, enjoy good neighbourly relations.'

People are never told that the reply from the Hamas bomb-making chief Mohammed Deif was instant. On the website of the Izz ad-Din al-Qassam Brigades he declared: 'I thank Allah the exalted for his support in the Jihad of our people. I ask for your assistance to our jihad... We shall not rest until our entire holy land is liberated

---

15 Palestinian Militants Ransack Former Gush Katif Greenhouses', Haaretz, 10 February, 2006.

... To the Zionists we promise that tomorrow all of Palestine will become hell for you.'

They do not know that in spite of the Hamas threats, Israel signed an Agreement on Movement and Access with the Palestinian Authority after leaving Gaza. This gave the Palestinians control over their own borders for the first time in history, allowed for imports and exports, and even raised the prospect of the construction of a seaport and discussions on an airport. But unfortunately, Hamas does not respect deals made between the PA and Israel.

They do not know that Hamas launched a coup against other Palestinians in 2007, took over the Strip, drove out its Palestinian political rival Fatah, threw Palestinians who opposed them from rooftops, and declared that, as the new rulers of Gaza, that they would now use the Strip as a base to destroy Israel.

They do not know that as a direct result, not only Israel but also Egypt put restrictions on the borders with Gaza to stop Hamas terrorism. Israel instituted a legal maritime blockade around Gaza to keep rockets and other weapons out of the hands of Hamas, while letting food and another humanitarian aid in.

They do not know that a UN inquiry (the 2011 Palmer Report) concluded that Israel's maritime blockade was legal given the threat it faced.

They do not know that in March 2014, Israel intercepted an Iranian ship, one of several intercepted by Israel, with a cargo of weapons for Hamas in Gaza, including advanced M-302 surface-to-surface missiles, showing again why the naval blockade is necessary.[16]

What you say about Hamas might be true but the children of Gaza are not being killed by Hamas. They are being killed by Israeli air strikes.

Israel didn't want any of the recent conflicts. War is never good for anyone. Israel supported every ceasefire proposal in

---

16   David Horovitz, 'Why are we fighting with Gaza, again?' Times of Israel, 8 July.

2014–including those proposed by Egypt and the Arab League – but Hamas refused to stop firing rockets on Israelis civilians.

Hamas's rockets are more potent now. Israelis no longer face the short-range and crude Qassam rockets fired by Hamas into Sderot in Israel in 2005. They face sophisticated Iranian-supplied Fajr-5, R-160 and M-302 rockets capable of reaching Tel Aviv and Jerusalem. In 2014 a Hamas rocket reached Zichron Ya'akov, 100 miles from Gaza.

90 per cent of Israel is now within range of rockets from Gaza. Israel has no choice but to try and reduce the threat to its citizens by restoring deterrence against Hamas rockets.

Israel's faces an excruciating dilemma: how to restore deterrence, how to use force against the terrorists of Gaza to stop rockets landing on the civilians of Israel, without that force endangering the civilians of Gaza.

Israel has developed three responses to this dilemma. Three ways to try as best it can in a complex combat situation to avoid innocent civilians being caught up in the crossfire. None are fool proof.

- First, intelligence. Each target is selected following long-term intelligence efforts indicating a direct link to terrorist infrastructure (rocket launchers, command and control, etc.).

- Second, warnings. Israel uses a variety of methods, each constantly refined, to avoid strikes causing civilian causalities. These methods include: leaflet drops, texting, phone calls to buildings, the use of pin point precision rockets, the use of the 'knock on the roof' tactic – where Israel deploys a 'bomb' which only makes a loud noise in order to warn civilians to leave the targeted area. Missions are aborted or altered, when they may cause civilian deaths, sometimes at huge cost to Israeli security.

- Third, self-limitation. Israel has deliberately limited its use of the range of awesome weaponry it has available.

The result was noted by former British Army Colonel Richard Kemp. A United   Nations study of the 2008-9 conflict between Israel and Hamas showed that 'that the ratio of civilian to combatant deaths in Gaza was by far the lowest in any asymmetric conflict in the history of warfare.' Kemp said that 'there has been an average three-to- one ratio of civilian to combatant deaths in such conflicts worldwide. Three civilians for every combatant killed. That is the estimated ratio in Afghanistan: three-to-one. In Iraq, and in Kosovo, it was worse: the ratio is believed to be four-to-one. Anecdotal evidence suggests the ratios were very much higher in Chechnya and Serbia. In Gaza, it was less than one-to-one.'

In the 2012 Gaza conflict, 1,600 Israeli strikes against long-range missiles and terror infrastructure caused 60-70 Palestinian civilian deaths.

Each victim matters. Each is a tragedy. But again, the ratio of combatant to non-combatant deaths was without precedent in modern warfare. Again, in 2014, Israel estimates that around half the Gaza's fatalities caused by the conflict were combatants.

So why, despite all these Israeli efforts, do civilians still die?

First, because of what the military theorist Carl von Clausewitz famously called 'the fog of war' – intelligence is always incomplete, sometimes mistaken, while soldiers and planners are not just subject to human limit like anyone else but have to act in a fevered and terrifying environment.

Second, because of the awesome destructive power of modern munitions, which means that their sustained use within in urban settings in which combatants and non- combatants are co-mingled, will always – despite every effort – produce civilian casualties.

Third, the fact that Hamas deliberately engineers the co-mingling of combatants and non-combatants. Hamas deliberately locates rockets in populated areas, inside housing complexes, mosques, hospitals and schools. Hamas have even encouraged Gazans not to heed IDF's warnings but to go up onto the roofs to prevent an air strike. Meanwhile Hamas commanders spent the 2014 conflict hiding in a bunker underneath Shifa hospital in Gaza.

The UN and the world community condemns all this. Why does Hamas continue to put Palestinian children in danger?[17]

But surely Israel's actions in Gaza have been disproportionate?

In international law and in 'just war' theory, proportionality is not the same thing   as symmetry. Princeton Professor Michael Walzer, author of the seminal study Just and Unjust Wars, puts it like this:

Proportionality doesn't mean 'tit for tat,' as in the family feud. The Hatfields kill three McCoys, so the McCoys must kill three Hatfields. More than three, and they are breaking the rules of the feud, where proportionality means symmetry.

The use of the term is different with regard to war, because war isn't an act of retribution; it is n't a backward-looking activity, and the law of even-Steven doesn't apply. Like it or not, war is always purposive in character; it has a goal, an end-in-view.

Israel's stated goal was simple, necessary and rightful: to protect the citizens of southern Israel by stopping the rocket attacks. The question Israel faced was: what level of force is necessary to stop these rockets? During the last conflict Israel kept pausing, proposing and accepting cease-fires. Hamas broke each one. It is against that fact, as well as the dangerous combination of the Hamas rocket threat and the Hamas ideology of genocidal hatred towards all Jews – and what that terrible combination may yet inflict upon over a million citizens of Israel in the line of rocket fire if deterrence is not restored – that the 'proportionality' of the Israeli efforts to restore deterrence must be judged.[18]

---

17 Alan Johnson, 'Gaza: the ethical dilemmas of fighting terrorism', Daily Telegraph, 12 July 2014.

18 Alan Johnson, 'Why Israel's action in Gaza is not "disproportionate"', New Statesman, 21 November 2012.

Why does Israel need to respond at all? When Norman Finkelstein came to campus, he told us that Hamas do not have rockets, they only have fireworks.

Norman Finkelstein, with all due respect to him, is simply wrong. Hamas have rockets not fireworks, and that is why Israel has no choice but to respond.

Yes, back in 2001, Qassam rockets fell on Sderot and nearby villages, a mere 1.5 kilometers from Gaza. But then came Qassam rockets with a maximum range of 3 to 4 kilometers. Soon upgraded, their range was 12 to 15 kilometers by 2005. Before long, the Israeli city of Ashkelon, 20 kilometers north of Gaza, with a population of 120,000, was a target. By 2006, Katyusha rockets made in Gaza were being fired 12 miles into Israel. More powerful Grad-type rockets were smuggled into Gaza from 2008 and were hitting the town of Netivot, 20 kilometers east of Gaza, and soon after that, KiryatGat and Beer Sheva, about twice as far away.

And then the Iranians began supplying Hamas with Fajr-5 rockets, smuggled through Sudan and Egypt, and they were capable of hitting Tel Aviv and the Jerusalem outskirts. By 2014, Hamas was firing Syrian-made M-302s and hitting Zichron Yaakov, around 160 kilometers, or about 100 miles, from Gaza.

The idea that Israel can simply ignore these rockets is simply not serious. By 2009, 15 Israeli civilians were dead from rocket fire and Fred Abrahams, the senior emergencies researcher at Human Rights Watch, was denouncing Hamas as guilty of war crimes, as more and more of southern Israel came under fire.

By 2009, Amnesty International was reporting that 1 million Israelis now lived in fear of rockets as Hamas and Palestinian Islamic Jihad fired on 'homes, businesses, schools, other public buildings, and vehicles in and around towns and villages in southern Israel'. Had Israel's not invested heavily in air raid shelters and the Iron Dome anti-missile system, Israeli casualties would have been significantly higher.

As Barack Obama said in July 2008 when he visited Sderot, an

Israeli town on the Gaza border, 'If somebody was sending rockets into my house where my two daughters sleep at night, I'm going to do everything in my power to stop that. And I would expect Israelis to do the same thing.'

Can't Israel rely on its 'Iron Dome' system to knock the Hamas rockets out of the sky?

Unfortunately, not.

For one thing, the success rate of Iron Dome, Israel's missile defense system, is not 100 per cent. That matters hugely because over 15,000 rockets and mortars have targeted Israel since 2001.

Some rockets get through and they kill Israelis. Aharon Smadga, Itzik Amsalem, and Mira Sharf (who was reportedly pregnant) were victims of a direct hit on their house in the Israeli town of Kiryat Malachi in 2012.

For another thing, you have to understand the impact of the rockets that don't get through. The sirens, the terror, the rushing to the bomb shelter – all have a profoundly traumatic impact on Israeli children.[19]

The city of Sderot in southern Israel, less than 2 kilometers from the Gaza Strip, first came under Palestinian rocket fire in 2001. Hamas would time the rockets to hit the school run. Between April 2001 and December 2008, more than 1,000 alarms were sounded in or near Sderot. By then, according to NATAL, the Israel Trauma Center for Victims of Terror and War, between 75 per cent and 94 per cent of Sderot children ages 4 to 18 were exhibiting symptoms of post-traumatic stress disorder(PTSD).

By 2008, 120 of Sderot's children were in long-term mental health therapy. 30 per cent of Sderot's one-to six-year-olds needed long-term psychological treatment and 60 per cent of infants refused to sleep alone. And – this is the crux of the matter – as the reach of the Hamas rockets has increased so has the number of Israeli children going through what the children of Sderot have gone

---

19 Alan Johnson, 'Hamas rockets traumatise Israeli children', World Affairs, 25 July 2014

through and are still going through.

No government can tolerate that.

This is a very different picture of Hamas than I get from the media.

Hamas has a long record of shutting down news bureaus, arresting reporters and cameramen, confiscating equipment and beating up journalists. That record has already been documented by the Committee to Protect Journalists.

In the 2014 conflict the Foreign Press Association (FPA) issued an astonishing protest about the 'blatant, incessant, forceful and unorthodox' intimidation of journalists in the Gaza Strip by Hamas. 'In several cases,' the FPA complained, 'foreign reporters working in Gaza have been harassed, threatened or questioned over stories'. The FPA said this amounted to 'denying readers and viewers an objective picture from the ground,' adding 'we are also aware that Hamas is trying to put in place a 'vetting' procedure that would, in effect, allow for the blacklisting of specific journalists. Such a procedure is vehemently opposed by the FPA.'[20]

But the Israelis have all the power. Palestinians have no choices so can't be held responsible for their actions. Surely, it's all down to the Israelis to sort this out?

Few ideas have done more damage to the prospects of building a realistic, genuine and enduring peace than this one.

It's time to stop infantilising the Palestinian government and Hamas.[21]

It is myth is that the Palestinian leaders are helpless, dominated by circumstance and driven by emotion, lacking all political choice, and below the age of responsibility. It is a myth that the Israelis are masters of all circumstances, rational and calculating,

20 Poll: Arabs Prefer Israel to Palestinian Authority. Israel Today, 25 November 2014.

21 Ali Haider, 'Arabs, the Israeli civil service needs you.' Haaretz, 16 August 2012.

the root cause of everything, and responsible for everything.

In reality this is an Orientalist view of the Palestinians, except that this time the Oriental Other is not disdained but affirmed as a noble savage. It's a bit racist, to be honest – the racism of low expectations.

For example, the former Liberal Democrat MP David Ward tweeted after the Jerusalem synagogue murderers of 2014– when Palestinian terrorists hacked rabbis at prayer to death as well as killing a Druze police officer–that the killers had been 'driven to madness', which not only removed the agency of Palestinians but also their sanity.

This infantilisation of the Palestinians completely distorts our understanding of the three things: the history of the conflict, Israel's security needs, and the reasons for the failure, thus far at least, of the peace process.

Getting History Wrong:

Infantilising the Palestinians distorts our understanding of the responsibility for the key turning points of the conflict such as the war of 1948, the 1967 war, the collapse of the Camp David peace talks in 2000, and what happened in Gaza after Israel left in 2005. The Palestinians are cast in each case as a people beyond the reach of judgement. Israel, and only Israel, is held to be blamed.

Getting Security Wrong:

The infantilisation of the Palestinians distorts our understanding of the threats to Israel's security. These threats are often simply discounted by western activists, as if they don't exist, as if they are made up, while the security measures taken by Israel to defend itself against these threats are framed as motiveless and cruel acts.

For example, the barrier initially planned and constructed in 2002 to keep out Palestinian suicide bombers who were killing Jews and Arabs is completely twisted into an 'Israeli Apartheid

Wall' built to segregate Jews from Arabs.

Getting the Peace Process Wrong:

Infantilising the Palestinians also warps our understanding of the reasons for the failure of the peace process thus far, because it excludes from consideration Palestinian rejectionism, terrorism, authoritarianism, Islamism, corruption and its promotion of a culture of incitement, demonization and anti-semitism. This infantilisation of the Palestinians does untold damage.

The Palestinians are allowed to take maximalist positions that make a final status agreement impossible. For example, Palestinian refusal to recognize the Jewish people's right to sel determination. For example, the Palestinians insist that not only the refugees of 1948-9, but also their children, grandchildren and great grandchildren 'return' to Israel, ensuring that Israel will become yet another Arab state – yet no one points out that these demands are an obstacle to the only viable peace: two-states for two peoples.

The Palestinians are allowed to reject one Israeli offer of statehood after another – Camp David, Annapolis – safe in the knowledge that people in the West will blame all-powerful Israel for the absence of a Palestinian state.

The Palestinian leaders are allowed to feed their population a diet of hate and incitement and receive unconditional aid from the international community.

As for Hamas, they can break every ceasefire in the summer of 2014 – even the ones they declared themselves! – they can locate rockets in hospitals, they can have their HQ in the basement of Shifa hospital, but few journalists will even mention any of this let alone criticise them for it.

Because they have been infantilised, Hamas can drop 875 rockets on Gazans – i.e. the rockets that didn't even make it out of the Strip in 2014 – knowing that no one will point that out.

Because they have been infantilised, 600,000 tons of cement can go to build terror tunnels instead of a vibrant, prosperous Gaza, and yet the aid keeps coming.

THE APRATHIED SMEAR

My lecturers tell me that Israel is an 'Apartheid state'. Is that true?

No. 'Apartheid' is the Dutch-Afrikaans term for separation, used to describe the   racial segregation and discrimination enforced violently by white minority governments on non-whites in South Africa from 1948 to 1994. Benjamin Pogrund, former anti-apartheid activist, deputy editor of the Rand Daily Mail, and a friend of Nelson Mandela said this: 'Applying the word 'apartheid' to Israelis is both factually wrong and politically naïve.'

We should listen to Pogrund. The 'apartheid' smear is factually wrong, politically polarising and it damages both the campus debate and, more importantly, the peace process. It should be dropped.[22]

Is there 'apartheid' for the 20 per cent of Israelis who are not Jewish?

No. Israel it is a thriving multi-ethnic democracy in which the Arab minority is guaranteed equal rights under the Basic Laws. All faiths vote and all enjoy freedom of worship. There are no legal restrictions on movement, employment, or sexual or marital relations. Universities and hospitals are integrated and the judiciary counters discrimination.

Israel's Arab citizens hold collective rights as a national minority. Israel is the only place in the Middle East where all minorities are protected. Its parliament has the widest and most far-reaching representation of voices.

Arabic is an official language and there is a thriving Arabic mass media, literature and theatre scene. An Arab Israel is it on the Israeli Supreme Court. 20 per cent of the students at the elite Technion University are Arabs. Israeli Arab infant mortality rates are better than those of the USA.

Although they are rightly very critical of a range of discriminations

---

22 Ofra Edelman, 'Katsav sentenced to 7 years. Haaretz, March 23 2011.

and inequalities, 77 per cent of the Arab citizens of Israel say that they prefer living in Israel to any other country in the world.[23]

Yes, Israel's Arab citizens suffer from a number of disadvantages but to use the term 'apartheid' to describe those disadvantages is ridiculous. There are 17 Arab MKs (MPs) in the current 120-member Knesset and they are among the government's harshest critics. The 'Joint List' – an alliance of four Arab-dominated parties – is the third largest party in the Knesset. Arabs have served in the Cabinet (e.g. RalebMajadele), in the civil service (7.8 per cent of civil servants in Israel are Arab)[24], and on the Supreme Court (Justice Salim Joubran). It was an Israeli Arab judge, George Karra, who sentenced former President of Israel, Moshe Katsav, to jail for seven years on a rape conviction.[25]

The infant mortality rate in Israel in 2011 was 3.5 deaths to 1000 live births – 2.8 for Jews and 3.7 for Arabs. That's unequal, yes, but the infant mortality rate for the Arab minority in Israel ranks equal or better than the rate for the majority in Europe and the United States. It is far better than the infant mortality rates in the surrounding Arab world.

Israeli governments have been pursuing policies to close the remaining economic gaps between the Jewish majority and the Arab minority by opening up the civil service, equalising welfare, introducing Arabic into Jewish schools, and improving access to higher education.

Writing in 2012 at the radical +972 website, Ron Gerlitz and Batya Kallus, the co- executivedirectorsofSikkuyanArab-Je wishorganisationworkingtoadvanceequality, argued that as a result of a government drive from above and pressure from below by Arab civil society, 'over the last ten years, the government has begun to initiate significant and innovative

---

23 Ron Gerlitz and Batya Kallus, 'A Dangerous Position'. +972, 19 October 2012.

24 Central Intelligence Agency, 2013 CIA World Factbook, Skyhorse Publishing, 2013.

25 Richard J. Goldstone, 'Israel and the Apartheid Slander'. New York Times, 21 October 2011.

processes to close the gaps of inequality, advance economic development, and promote employment for the Arab population.'

In 2016 Sikkuy hailed the Government's 5-year Arab Economic Development Plan as 'historic'.

But isn't there apartheid on the West Bank?

Since 1967 Israel has occupied the West Bank after winning the Six Day War, a pre- emptive war of self-defence against the Arab armies that were once again massed on its borders, intent on 'driving the Jews into the sea'.

The occupation persists 49 years later not because Israel wants to rule over the territories but because peace talks – in which Israel seeks recognition and security guarantees in return for the creation of Palestinian state in the Gaza Strip and West Bank– have failed thus far. That is why the occupation continues, not because Israelis running a permanent 'apartheid' regime.

The Palestinian population in the Territories has continued to expand rapidly.

According to the UN, the total Palestinian population in Gaza, the West Bank, and East Jerusalem was 1,094,000 in 1970, 2,152,000 in 1990, and now stands at 4.4 million.[26]

Judge Richard Goldstone a former Justice of the South African Constitutional Court, who led the United Nations fact-finding mission on the Gaza conflict of 2008-9, objected strongly to the Apartheid smear: '[In the West Bank] there is no intent to maintain "an institutionalised regime of systematic oppression and domination by one racial group" [the definition of apartheid under the 1998 Rome Statute]. South Africa's enforced racial separation was intended to permanently benefit the white minority, to the detriment of other races. By contrast, Israel has agreed to the existence of a Palestinian state in Gaza and almost all of the West Bank, and is calling for the Palestinians to negotiate

---

26 Ehud Olmert, 'Olmert: Two-state solution is crucial to Israel as a Jewish and democratic state'. Haaretz, 28 April 2013.; Tzipi Livni, 'Livni to Post: I have unfinished business in making peace with Palestinians'.

the parameters.'[27]

Exactly.

United Nations Security Council Resolution 242, passed in the wake of the Six Day War, and accepted by Israel, calls for peace to be based on two principles: '(i) Withdrawal of Israel armed forces from territories occupied in the recent conflict;

The termination of all claims or states of belligerency.' In other words, Israel is expected to relinquish territory whilst the Arab states are expected to recognise Israel's right to exist peacefully in the region. 242 did not call for immediate and total Israeli withdrawal from all of the Territories but established that the basis for peace was these two principles.

Since 1967, the Israeli presence in Gaza and the West Bank has been the subject of entirely legitimate criticism (much of it coming from within Israel itself, including from Israeli Prime Ministers, Ministers, security chiefs, and intellectuals).[28]Israel has a moral responsibility to do all it can to avoid human rights abuses and to end the occupation   as soon as possible, but it also has a responsibility to do the latter in a way that does   not endanger the lives and future of its own citizens, or bring about the circumstances for an even worse conflict. That is Israel's dilemma. It seeks to resolve that dilemma by negotiations to establish two-states for two peoples.

What about the 'apartheid wall' built to keep Arabs away from Jews? That sure sounds like apartheid!

Many of the measures taken by Israel in the Territories that are labelled 'apartheid' – the so-called 'apartheid wall' for example – are actually security measures.

---

27 Jerusalem Post, 21 October 2013.; Yuval Diskin, 'Diskin: Israel nears point of no return on two-state solution'. Jerusalem Post, 13 July 2013; Amos Oz, 'Amos Oz slams West Bank "occupation"', Ynet, 21 June 2011.

28 Ido Rosenzweig and Prof. Yuval Shany, 'A Decade of Palestinian Terrorism – Report by the IsraeliSecurity Agency'. The Israeli Democracy Institute.

The barrier – 90 per cent of which is actually a fence – was not built to separate Jews from Arabs because of racism. It was built to protect Jews and Arabs from Palestinian suicide bombers. There are both Jews and Arabs living on both sides of it.

Simona Rodin was 18 when, on 1 June 2001 she went to the Dolphinarium discotheque in Tel Aviv. So, did Said Khutari, who travelled from the West Bank town of Qalqilya with a deadly mix of powerful explosives and hundreds of steel ball bearings strapped to his chest. In the Disco, at 11:26 p.m. he blew himself up, murdering Simona and 20 other youngsters, and injuring 132.

This was the Second Intifada–a wave of Palestinian suicide bombings and other terrorist attacks on Israel. By 2002, a fatal suicide bombing was carried out in Israel nearly every two weeks on average. In just three years, over 900 Israeli civilians were killed and 6000 injured by terrorism coming from West Bank.[29]

The barrier worked.

It was not the only factor, but it was an important factor in achieving a fall of more than 90 per cent in the number of attacks and 70 per cent in the number of Israelis murdered, from an average of 103 slain per year before the barrier to 28 after its construction. Those are real lives, saved. And those lives must be allowed to enter into our moral calculus and into our attitude towards the barrier.

Israel calls itself a 'Jewish state.' Doesn't that mean it discriminates against non-Jews?

The term 'Jewish state' is misunderstood. 'Jewish', in this context, refers to a people not a religion. It does not mean that Israel is a theocracy (rule by clerics) or a state exclusively for Jews. Israel is a democracy (rule by the people), governed by the rule of law as drafted by an elected parliament, the Knesset. All faiths vote and enjoy freedom of worship.

'Jewish state' just means that Israel is the national homeland for

29 Abid

the Jewish people with citizenship, civic equality and minority rights for its non-Jews. 'The homeland of the Jewish people' is a more accurate and more helpful phrase.

Israel is a nation-state. There are many of those in the world. Tal Becker, the Israeli lawyer and peace-negotiator under the Annapolis process in 2007-8, puts it most clearly: 'When we say Israel is a Jewish state, we mean that it is the national home of the Jewish people, where the Jewish people realise their right to self-determination. The Jewish people realising their right to self-determination is not a principle that is contrary to democracy. It is a universal legal principle.'

But Israeli Jews wish to preserve a 'Jewish majority' in Israel. Isn't that a form of racism towards non-Jews?

No. It is not unusual that one community is the majority within a nation-state and seeks to maintain that status. In fact, this is true in nearly every country in the world.

Moreover, societies usually reflect the cultural identity of the majority. India and Pakistan were established at the same time as Israel, but no one believes these nations are illegitimate because one is predominantly Hindu and the other Muslim, or because the laws and customs of each country – from the role of Islam in Pakistan to the treatment of cows as sacred in India – reflect those majorities.

Many states define their immigration policies based on their own specific context, history and ethnic or national character. As Gil Troy and Martin J. Raffel point out 'The German constitution offers automatic citizenship to refugees and displaced persons of German ethnic origin from the former Soviet Union and Eastern Europe – individuals who for many generations had no geographic or civic relationship with the state. Greece's citizenship law confers special advantages on ethnic Greeks, including dispensing with the residency requirement for naturalization purposes.

Finland repatriates ethnic Finns from the former Soviet Union. In Poland, anyone whose Polish origin is confirmed in accordance with its constitution may settle permanently in that country. The Irish nationality law empowers the Ministry of Justice to grant an exemption from naturalisation prerequisites when the applicant is of Irish descent or Irish associations.[30]

The 'Law of Return' grants a Jew from anywhere in the world an automatic right to become an Israeli citizen. This right is not enjoyed by non-Jews. Isn't that apartheid?

No.

In every generation throughout its history, the Jewish people have suffered persecution and expulsion. This situation culminated in the Holocaust, a genocide from which the Jews of Europe found no place of refuge. One of the primary goals of the Zionist movement was to create one state in the world, which would be a national home for the Jewish people, and a refuge by definition open to Jewish immigration.

When the State of Israel was founded in 1948, one of its most urgent challenges was to absorb hundreds of thousands of stateless Jewish refugees who had been forced from their homes and lost everything in the Holocaust. At the same time, it had to absorb over 850,000 Jews who fled rising persecution or were expelled from Arab and Muslim lands after the 1948 War of Independence.

Israel duly passed a law – The Law of Return – which granted the right of citizenship to any Jew who wished to live in Israel. Whilst the traditional religious definition of a Jew is someone who has a Jewish mother, the law of return takes a broader definition. In Nazi Germany, individuals were murdered as Jews if they had even one Jewish grandparent, and that is why the State of Israel defines a Jew for the purposes of the right of return as anyone with one Jewish grandparent. The principle is that anyone who could be persecuted for being Jew is thought to have the right of refuge.

---

30 Gil Troy and Martin J. Raffel, Israel: Jewish and Democratic, Jewish Federations of North America, 2013

And the sad truth – which a cursory look at the daily papers, will confirm – is that anti-semitism has not gone away, and there is still a need for the Law of Return.

Author's meeting with Former Vice Prime Minister and Foreign
Minister of Israel, **Tzipi Livni**

Author's meeting with Former Mossad Director, **Shabtai Shavit**

Author's Meeting with Former Head of Analysis Division in
Military Intelligence of Israel, **General Yosef Kuperwasser**

Author's meeting with Former Chief Supernatant, Shin Bet,
Israeli Security Agency, **Asher Ben Artzi**

BIBLIOGRAPHY

1. Ephraim Karsh, 2008, Islamic Attitude to Israel

2. Shlomo Sand, 2010, The Invention of the Jewish People

3. Dave Rich, 2016, The Left's Jewish Problem

4. Robin Shepherd, 2009, A State Beyond the Pale, Europe's Problem with Israel

5. Gideon Levy, 2010, The Punishment of Gaza

6. Martin Bunton, 2013, The Palestinian Israel Conflict

7. Mossab Hassab Yousef, 2010, Son of Hamas

8. Tarek Fatah, 2010, The Jew is not My Enemy

9. Alan Dershowitz, 2014, Terror Tunnels: The case of Israel's just war against Hamas

10. Zaki Chehab, 2007, Inside Hamas: The Untold Story of Militants, Martyrs and Spies

11. Gordon Thomas, 2009, Gideon's Spies: The Secret History of the Mossad

12. Michael Ross, 1988, The Volunteer, The Secret Life of the Mossad

13. Alan Dershowitz. 2003, The Case for Israel

14. Barry Shaw, 2011, Israel Reclaiming the Narrative

15. Oded Hakalia, 2015, Settlers in Contested Lands

16. Uri Milstein, 2012, The birth of a Palestinian Nation: The

Myth of the Deir Yassin Massacre

17. Alan Dershowitz, 2009, The Case for Moral Clarity: Israel, Hamas and Gaza

18. Ronen Bergman, 2018, Rise and Kill First: The Secret History of Israel's Targeted Assassinations

19. Jonathan Sacks, 2015, Not in God's Name: Confronting Religious Violence

20. Richard A. Burridge, 2018, Confronting Religious Violence: A Counter Narrative

21. Nitsana Darshan-Leitner, 2017, Harpoon: Inside the Covert War Against Terrorism's Money Masters

22. Reuters, 2002, The Israeli-Palestinian Conflict: Crises in the Middle East

23. Boaz Ganor, 2008, The Counter Terrorism Puzzle: A Guide for Decision Makers

24. Moshe Yegar, 2007, Pakistan and Israel: Jewish Political Studies Review

25. George Crile, 2007, Charlie Wilson's War

26. P R Kumaraswamy 2000, Beyond the Veil: Israel Pakistan Relations

27. IMFA, 2017, Jewish refugees expelled from Arab lands and from Iran

28. Abu-Abdullah Al-Atharee, 2010, The Rise of Jihadist Extremism in the West

29. IMFA, 2016, Behind the Lines: Facts and Figures – Islam In Israel

30. Yaroslav Trofimov, 2008, The Siege of Makkah: The Forgotten Uprising in Islam's Holiest Shrine

31. Airf Jamal, 2014, Call for Transnational Jihad

32. Michael L. Rodkinson. 2009, The Babylonian Talmud

33. The Quran (The Holy Book of Islam)

34. Ephraim Karsh. 2017, The Real Story: An inevitable conflict - The Six-Day War

35. The Sahih Bukhari (The Book of Ahadith, Sayings of the Prophet of Islam)

36. Abdul Hadi Palazzi, 2009, What the Qur'an really says

37. Professor Alan Johnson, 2016, Israel and The Palestine: A Guide to the Debate

INDEX

ABOUT THE AUTHOR

Mr. Noor Dahri is the Founder and Executive Director of Islamic Theology of Counter Terrorism- ITCT, a UK based Counter Islamist Terrorism Think Tank. Noor was born and raised in Pakistan. He was an active member of Lahskar -e-Taibah (LeT), a Jihadist organisation in Pakistan. Noor Dahri has also worked with the London Police department for the last seven years. He has studied Forensics and Criminal Psychology from Oxford – UK, Counter Terrorism from the University of Maryland – U.S.A and also studied Counter Terrorism from International Institute for Counter Terrorism ICT- Israel. He is an independent researcher in Counter Islamist Terrorism and Islamist Extremism.

Mr. Dahri has written many research articles on the hot issues such as Counter Terrorism, Violent Extremism, De-Radicalisation and Israel-Palestine conflict which have been published in various newspapers. Noor has attended many events, conferences on the threat of Counter Terrorism and also visited many institutes and libraries. Noor is a Middle East Analyst at The Great Middle East and a regular contributor at the Times of Israel (Israel) and The Daily Times (Pak). He has appeared on numerous TV and Radio shows for his interviews.

Noor is a first Pakistani, who has been officially invited to deliver his speeches at the International Institute for Counter Terrorism -ICT in Israel on the topic of "From Daw'ah To Jihad: Breaking the Radicalization and Violent Cycle". Mr. Noor is the fellow member of the Intelligence Community USA and a member of the security think tank Henry Jackson society UK. He regularly attends discussion-based events in the House of Commons and the House of Lords (UK Parliaments). He has visited many countries for his research work.

Noor Dahri received a "Life Achievement Award Certificate" by Lord Frank Judd at The House of Lords- London in 2017.

He has authored the book: *Global Jihad, Islamic Radicalisation and Counter Strategy* that was published from India in 2019.